SEXUALITY IN OVERDRIVE?

Exploring Desire, Identity, and Excess

SEXUALITY IN OVERDRIVE?

Exploring Desire, Identity, and Excess

Vicente "Tex" S. Hernandez

Polaris Publishing

Manila, 2026

© 2026 Vicente Javier Stabile Hernandez
All rights reserved.

First Edition, October 25, 2024.

Second Edition

No part of this publication may be reproduced, duplicated, or transmitted in any form—electronic or printed—without prior written permission from the author. Recording of this work is strictly prohibited.

Image Credits.

Unless otherwise indicated, the images in this book were created using AI-assisted rendering tools, guided by the author's conceptual and compositional direction. These visuals serve as symbolic companions to the text, reflecting its philosophical and emotional themes.

This title—along with related articles and forthcoming works in the series—can be found at echoepolaris.com, echoesofpolaris.com, or by searching for it in Google Play Books or the Amazon Kindle Store.

The Google Play Books and Amazon Kindle Store edition is published under the title *Shall I Dress It? Sexuality in Overdrive*.

Printed and distributed by Amazon KDP.

I've got the magic in me.

Every time I touch that track, it turns into gold

Now everybody knows I've got the magic, magic, magic.

CeeLo Green, B.o.B., Rivers Cuomo (*Pitch Perfect*)

Contents

Introduction 1
Chapter One: Fashion 5
    Contemporary Fashion 9
    Margaret Sanger 11
    Alfred Kinsey 16
    Hugh Hefner 19
Chapter Two: The Pornographic Psyche 21
    Sexual Grooming 23
    The Matrix 25
    The Brain 28
    The Drug 32
        Withdrawal and Detox 33
Chapter Three: It's Complicated 35
    Constructivism and Postmodernism 37
        Disassociation from Reality 40
    The Scientific Claims 43
        The Homosexual Chromosome 43
        External Agents 44
        Mutations 46

- Lobbying Groups 47
- Abuse 48
  - Pornography 49
  - Traumatic Sexual Experiences 50
- Cultural Factors 52
  - School Regulations 52
  - Home and the Environment 55
  - Personality Profiles 57

Chapter Four: Intimacy's Hack 61
- The Contraceptive Mentality 62
- Exploring Stimuli and Desire 67
- Sexy Looks 70
- Parading Intimacy 72
- A Human Right 76
- True Love vs. Self-Love 79
  - Complementarity 81

Chapter Five: The Broken Jar 85
- Repairs 87
- The Magic in Me 91
- Magical 93

Chapter Six: We Need Answers 97
- The Sexual Liberation of Women 97
- The Contraceptive Mentality 99
- The Sexual Revolution 102

Homosexuality	105
Magic	107
Conclusion	109
About the Author	111
Other Works by the Author	113
Notes	115

Introduction

Alejandro Colomar, a 29-year-old naturalist and computer scientist, chose to go naked during his regular routines in Aldaia, a town in the Valencia region of Spain. Not surprisingly, the neighborhood's reaction regarded Colomar's obsession as disturbing; apparently, he was insulted and even physically threatened.

When called to present himself to the regional court, he made headlines by appearing completely nude. After arrest, he declared his right to defend himself in the public courts and challenged the Spanish justice system, demanding his right to freedom of expression.

He said he intended to assert his right to practice *naturism*, which he believes is legal. Colomar argued that *naturism*, a philosophy that promotes bareness as a connection to nature, differs from *nudism* which is simply about physical nudity. He maintained that this philosophy granted him the right to forgo clothing— even in winter.

His case was passed on from the regional to the Supreme Court which ended up giving him the right to go naked along the streets of Aldaia. Colomar's actions have sparked discussions about nudity and its legal boundaries not only in Spain but beyond its borders.[1]

Opinions about nudism have often caused heated controversies, brought about by the proliferation of nudist beach resorts during the summer months—which began to take shape in the 1950s and 1960s—especially in the South of Europe.

After all, the naturist movement had emerged earlier. By 1903, the first naturist club was established in Germany—the FKK or Freikörperkultur—which flared the spreading of the movement to other European countries, including France and the Netherlands.[2]

Alejandro's attitude and the debates he sparked highlight the complexities many faces in grasping the differences between human and animal sexuality today. There is an overwhelming focus on sensuality, often manifesting in the trap of pornography, a surge in rape cases, escalating issues related to sex trafficking, health problems from emerging sexually transmitted diseases, a growing mistrust in marriage, and a declining interest in having children.

Amid this confusion, Colomar's late statement—'I am going to show them that I can go like this and since they bother me, I bother them'[3]—shows that there is certain lucidity and even intellectual clarity in his attitude: he is aware of 'bothering' others. Why?

Answers are not easy to find but when given, they might be difficult to accept. This book offers views, supported by reasons, that differ from what the media, lobbying groups, and popular opinions understand about contraception, pornography, homosexuality, love, complementarity, and intercourse. Responses to concrete opposing arguments are found in Chapter Five, 'We Need Answers'—which might not give the expected assessment, but it will surely enlighten your understanding.

Are fashion trends imposed on us? Do they reflect today's views on sexuality? Is there any connection between fashion trends and historical facts related to the development of the contraceptive mentality? Is the moral code a bit dated? Who are the masters of the new ethical code? Is pornography bizarre? Does pornography influence the brain's normal functioning? Are there alternative views on same-sex attraction?

Let me recommend an open-minded approach to your reading on these issues. If your strong beliefs and convictions don't leave room for opinion, please move on and don't waste your time and money. Thank you very much.

Chapter One: Fashion

You don't need to watch a fashion show to realize that your retro looks are history. Window shopping will tell you about it even if you don't plan to buy anything immediately. Storefront displays often showcase the latest fashion collections, giving an insight into new designs and seasonal trends. Fashion mirrors the cultural and ideological trajectory of every generation.

No one knows for certain what Neanderthals wore, but it's been suggested that they might have worn furs from the animals that they hunted. Hides with decorative designs are first traced back 2.6 million years.

Art has often given clues about fashion from the past. As the better-known civilizations like the Egyptian, the Greek, and the Roman left so much art and culture behind, it is easy to analyze their taste through fashion. Ancient Egyptians showcased their social status through clothing. Ancient Greeks embraced draped garments—the chiton, fastened at the shoulders, was their signature style—and sandals which were also popular. And Roman Fashion, influenced by Greek styles, featured luxurious trends.[4]

Many other early cultures reflect their dressing styles in pottery, religious symbolism, historical records from their dynasties, and monuments. These are often found in the Sumerian, Assyrian, Babylonian, Chinese, Harappan (Indu Valley), Minoan, Inca, Aztec, and less, but not the least, in the Caral Supe (Peru) Cultures.

Fig. 1. Ancient Sumerian, Egyptian, Greek, and Roman fashion.

There are remnants of other civilizations that predate the Sumerians, the first known civilization emerging around 6,000 years ago. However, their destruction by a cataclysm—whose nature is not yet fully understood—remains a mystery.

If antiquity left hardly a memory but artifacts, Medieval fashion, on the contrary, imprinted a cultural heritage in every emerging country around the world. Almost every nation today takes pride in a heritage rooted in the late Medieval traditions of their respective regions.

Without the Internet, telephone, or television, medieval fashion shows to a certain extent some common patterns in remote areas and isolated continents.

The Chinese hanfu, Japanese kimono, Indian sari, and Persian kaftan became prominent symbols of fashion together with the East African kanga and kikoi, the kente cloth in West Africa, and the North African djellaba. Medieval European fashion preferred tunics and gowns, hose and mantles, surcoats and cotehardies, leather shoes and boots.[5]

Fig. 2. The Chinese hanfu (woman), Japanese kimono (man), Indian sari (woman), Persian kaftan (man), East African kanga (woman) and West African kente (man).

Why is it that every emerging culture felt the need to adorn their bodies with headwear, various accessories, and intricate designs in the clothing they wore? Why is it that men and women from almost

8—Fashion

every religion or cultural background favor long, loose, or more fitted outer garments?

It seems that human nature called for it.

Animals don't dress up, cook their food, live in modern houses, write books, or manufacture computers.

The earliest record—explaining our human behavior—appears in the book of Genesis, where God, after the incident in the garden, asked Adam and Eve, "Who told you that you were naked? Have you eaten from the tree that I commanded you not to eat from?"[6]

Fig. 3. "Who told you that you were naked?"

Alejandro Colomar, our protagonist from the Introduction, was mistaken. Going about naked

contradicts human nature and leads to behaviors that are unhealthy for us.

Contemporary Fashion

Today, the old but rich fashion heritage has largely been overshadowed by an international phenomenon known as 'contemporary fashion.' It's captivating to see how various merging influences across borders are driven by modern trends and ideological factors that have shaped women's attire in a distinctive way

Modern inventions open the way to variety and fast-paced changes. "In 1856, teenager William Perkin accidentally discovered a dye he called mauve while trying to make quinine in his home lab. This accident spawned a new synthetic dye industry that changed the course of the textile industry turning them away from the use of natural dyes to producing dyes from coal tar."[7] Until then, the more common textiles were cotton, linen, wool, silk, and hemp.

The invention of the sewing machine is a little more complicated, but its contribution significantly accelerated the evolution of fashion. Attributed to different people, "the first machine to combine all the disparate elements of the previous half-century of innovation into the modern sewing machine was the device built by English inventor John Fisher in 1844, a little earlier than the very similar machines built by Isaac Merritt Singer in 1851, and the lesser-known Elias Howe, in 1845."[8]

Throughout the 20th century, women's outfits evolved dramatically. The Edwardian era (1901 to 1910) gave way to the flapper era of the 1920s and later, to the more practical way of dressing brought about by the Great Depression and World War II. "The "New Look" by Dior in 1947 reintroduced femininity with cinched waists and full skirts."[9]

Fig. 4. From the Edwardian era to the flapper years, through practical dressing and into the contemporary period—miniskirts, hippie, disco, punk, and minimalist culture.

However, the defiant spirit reflected in contemporary women's fashion began in the 1960s bringing about the so-called sexual revolution. This transforming era marked the dawn of modern fashion, defined by miniskirts and striking patterns, which profoundly shaped the latter half of the twentieth century. The hippie, disco, and punk culture was soon to invite more eclectic and extravagant styles ending up in the casual wear and minimalist look of the 1990's.

The evolution of fashion in the 20th century is not an accident. It resulted from cultural shifts and the technological advancements introduced by major social and ideological movements. Like in any other historical era, it mirrored the ideological trends that continue to shape the world today.

In the 21st Century, "Fashion has become more inclusive and diverse, with a mix of styles from various decades. Sustainable fashion and ethical practices are gaining importance. Technology and social media have also played a significant role in shaping trends."[10]

Tracing every ideology sprouting from the intellectual circles of history is too ambitious for a book like this. We will focus on introducing the key protagonists and examine how earlier trends influenced them. Using the analogy of an orchestra, the symphonic ideology in modern society emerges like music from the coordinated effort of each artist. Current trends are better understood by highlighting the individual contributions of each player.

Margaret Sanger

One of the greatest influencers of the 20th century has been Margaret Sanger (1879 – 1966). Margaret excelled in her persistent and pragmatic approach to problem-solving. She relied trustfully on the new ideas she picked up along the way. Unfortunately, this reliance lacked a solid intellectual foundation. As we might soon conclude, she misunderstood the significance and impact of her efforts.

As a nurse around 1910 to 1911, Sanger encountered numerous working-class immigrant women who often experienced multiple pregnancies, miscarriages, and self-induced abortions. One woman, Sadie Sachs, particularly stood out when Sanger was called to assist her during a severe illness resulting from a self-induced abortion. Following her recovery, Margaret pleaded with the attending physician for advice to avoid a similar situation in the future. The doctor's recommendation was for Sadie to practice abstinence.

A few months later, Margaret decided to forgo her work as a nurse when called back to Sadie's apartment. Sadie died shortly after Sanger's arrival because of another attempted self-induced abortion. According to Margaret, the issue was a lack of information on how to avoid unwanted pregnancy. For Margaret, this was a social problem about women's choices.

As the daughter of an Irish immigrant who proclaimed to be an atheist, she was radical, hard-headed, strongly influenced by self-ruling ideas, and talented. Margaret was the receiving end of century-old controversies brought about by Friedrich Hegel's (1770-1831) ideas on history as *progression from lower to higher forms*. Hegel's philosophy, particularly his dialectical method and the notion of absolute spirit suggested that history and reality are evolving processes that can transcend individual moral frameworks. This perspective led some to argue that moral absolutes have become relative in the face of historical development. His ideas would influence Karl Marx, Charles Darwin, Thomas Robert Malthus, and others who discarded all moral values and questioned ethics.

Fig. 5. **Margaret Sanger**
(Underwood & Underwood, Library of Congress Prints and Photographs Division, LC-USZ62-29808. Public domain. Courtesy of Wikimedia Commons).

Motivation turned Margaret from a spectator to a ruthless activist. She found in social organizations the channels that she needed for her campaign which now centered on the promotion of contraception. She searched for involvement in left-wing associations, and collaboration with local intellectuals and artists who reasoned like her.[11] Through them, she discovered that her best tools in the new populist, progressive United States were writing and lobbying.

She started to write regularly as a columnist under the titles 'What Every Mother Should Know' (1911–12) and 'What Every Girl Should Know' (1912–13) for the socialist magazine *New York Call*. "Sanger came to believe that only by liberating women from the risk of unwanted pregnancy would fundamental social change take place... In 1914, Sanger launched The Woman Rebel, an eight-page monthly newsletter that promoted contraception using the slogan 'No Gods, No Masters.' Sanger, collaborating with anarchist friends, popularized the term 'birth control.'"[12]

'No Gods, No Masters' is a fervent proclamation that abandons any anchor on moral or ethical principles leaving the person adrift in his or her understanding. Nobody can tell anyone what is good or bad, but in the assertion of one's own beliefs, he or she turns into the new Master. Margaret became the new Master of her generation and of the generations to come.

In August 1914, Margaret Sanger was indicted for violating postal obscenity laws by sending The Woman Rebel through the postal system. Rather than stand trial, she fled the country. Her contacts abroad guided her towards Neo-Malthusianism.

Back in the US in 1916, she openly fought the system establishing the first-ever family planning and birth control clinic. It was only in 1918 that the birth control movement won a victory through Judge Frederick E. Crane of the New York Court of Appeals who issued a ruling which allowed doctors to prescribe contraception. From then on, and through her campaigns, she managed to open a new birth control clinic, get funding from the Rockefeller Foundation, spread her ideas abroad, and make her population control programs as familiar as possible to people all over the world.

Margaret was not alone in her campaign for contraception. Emma Goldman (1869 – 1940) and Mary Dennett (1872 – 1947) echoed her claims together with women in other parts of the world like Marie Stopes (1880 – 1958) in the United Kingdom and Aletta Jacobs (1854 – 1929) in the Netherlands. Sigmund Freud (1856-1939) in Austria had just developed his theory of psychoanalysis which would strongly influence the research and the conclusions of scientists and eventually, control the intellectual circles.[13]

Contraceptive ideas have never been promoted to this extent before. Could the contraceptive mentality be linked to the fashion turns of the twentieth century, the sexual revolution of the 60's, and more, to the increasing divorce rates, the discarding of marriage as unreliable, the open hostilities against traditional family values, and even the gender ideology?

Further exploration will follow in the next chapters, but nobody would question contraception's role in sparking the cultural drift of the twentieth and twenty-first centuries. Contraception was inspired in the amoral mind of key players, supported by scientific hypothesis, and spread by the wealthiest, self-confident, and all-knowable tycoons. They tell us there are no rulers, no one to judge you, and no universal moral model—only the moral laws set by the key players. And, oh dear, you are left to navigate this on your own.

There is still a gap in our understanding. These are the radical extremes that we observe in society today such as perversity and abuse, pornographic degradation, the effort to make the unnatural natural, and the endless list of abnormalities welcomed by some who no longer see them as sicknesses but as advancements.

Alfred Kinsey

In the frontline of this influence, we find the life and research of Alfred Kinsey (1894 –1956), famous for coining the phrase, 'There is no abnormality and no normality.' Alfred was an American entomologist, psychologist, and the first sexologist.

Alfred became a student of applied biology at Harvard, where he studied under William Morton Wheeler, an eminent field biologist. He obtained a Doctoral Degree in Science after his meticulous Darwinian case study of the evolutionary taxonomy of the gall wasp in 1919 and became a full professor in 1929. In 1938, he agreed to lead a team-taught course on marriage where he illustrated lectures on the biology of sexual stimulation.

"Kinsey now shifted his research focus as well, transferring his obsessive concern with variation among gall wasps to the varieties of human sexual experience... Kinsey was using the marriage course to 'transform his private struggle against Victorian morality into a public crusade.'"[14] Funded by the Rockefeller Foundation, he established the Institute for Sex Research (1947), and today the Kinsey Institute for Research in Sex, Gender, and Reproduction.

Fig. 6. **Alfred Charles Kinsey**
(Photo by Unknown, Mondadori Publishers, Public Domain, via Wikimedia Commons).

His first publication made "the best-seller list within 3 weeks, despite its 804 pages, generally dry scientific style, and ponderous weight of statistics, tables, and graphs. By mid-March, it had sold 200,000 copies. The book, based on over 5000 sexual histories, provided a series of revelations about the prevalence of masturbation, adulterous sexual activity, and homosexuality."¹⁵ His controversial research—which included pedophiles, prostitutes, perverts, serial rapists, sex murderers, experiments involving the Institute's staff, and his personal experience—is regarded by many as the precursor to the sexual revolution of the 1960s and 1970s.¹⁶

There is a notable connection between Alfred Kinsey and Playboy magazine. Alfred Kinsey's research on human sexuality had a significant influence on Hugh Hefner, the founder of Playboy. Hefner was inspired by Kinsey's work to create a publication that would challenge societal norms and promote a more open discussion about sexuality. Hefner mentioned in the first issue of Playboy that the magazine aimed to fill a publishing need that was only slightly less important than the one addressed by the Kinsey Reports.¹⁷

Kinsey's research helped to pave the way to the extreme and bizarre sexual behavior that continues to challenge societal norms today as in the past. Such an influence is found, for example, in Kinsey's pedophile inclinations.

"James Jones, a Kinsey biographer (and admirer), in an interview for the 1998 British documentary Kinsey's Pedophiles, says, 'Kinsey in that chapter himself gives pretty graphic descriptions of their response to what he calls sexual stimulation. If you read those words, what he's talking about is kids who are screaming. Kids who are protesting in every way they can the fact that their bodies or their persons are being violated.' How many kids? According to Kinsey, 1,888 infants and young boys. This was child rape. This was child torture. This was criminal."[18]

Hugh Hefner

Playboy magazine played a significant role in popularizing Alfred Kinsey's ideas on human sexuality. The magazine continued to feature articles and interviews that discussed Kinsey's findings, making his research more accessible to a new public, and contributing to broadening the reach of the sexual revolution initiated in the 1960s.

Fig. 7. **Kinsey and Hef**
(Cartoon by Ben R. Daws, from *The Spectator*, based on commentary by Mark Powell).

Overall, the magazine was instrumental in bringing Kinsey's research to a wider audience, thereby shaping modern attitudes towards sexuality.[19]

20—Fashion

"A couple of weeks ago, the human face of the modern sexual revolution, Hugh Hefner died in the Playboy mansion in Holmby Hills, Los Angeles, at the age of 91. Although Hefner seemed to be the front man of this movement, actually the person in the vanguard of America's sexual awakening was the academic, Alfred Kinsey. Hefner was nothing more than Kinsey's pamphleteer and publicist. He was, in effect the 'great evangelist' for Kinsey's radical moral revisionism."[20]

Chapter Two: The Pornographic Psyche

The historical facts sketched in the previous chapter suggest that the drift towards an amoral—understood as unrestricted—sexual behavior is rooted in the contraceptive mentality. The slogan of Margaret, 'No Gods, no Masters,' has turned a human value—sexuality as a gift—into a valuable commodity. The commercial side of sex exploited as prostitution was not new in history but limited and restricted. The difference now is that thanks to contraceptives, all sexual fantasies are possible and justifiable. According to the new slogans, sexual pleasure has been liberated to become the focus and the objective of every relationship. And if having sex is the only important and crudest value, pornography is welcome and justifiable too.

Today, sex is prominently featured in movies, celebrated in various musical styles, exploited in advertising, and often seen as the ultimate value in relationships. The frustration that arises when sex is absent or unattainable is palpable. Because of this, many people—including medical doctors—consider pornography harmless; some would even recommend it to relieve stress.

Ignorance—or perhaps voluntary blindness—brings people to believe that pornography is inconsequential. No relevance is given to facts like the addiction of thousands over thousands to porn, the alarming number of sexual offenders, the gender disorientation experienced by many, the humiliation of feeling abnormal, and the increasing social isolation brought about by queer behavior.

"Existing studies do find that frequency of porn viewing correlates with depression, anxiety, stress, and social malfunctioning, as well as less sexual and relationship satisfaction and altered sexual tastes."[21]

There's a lot of scientific research looking at how pornography use might shape people's behavior—how it interacts with the brain, influences cognitive patterns, and affects things like aggression, sexual expectations, and the risk of abusive behavior. But the overall picture is complicated. Some websites offer users to share personal insights, proving that no matter what, pornography damages in one way or another the psyche of the person.

Where the research becomes more consistent is with violent pornographic material. When the content is aggressive—and especially when it feels realistic or immersive—there's a clearer link to more aggressive sexual attitudes and, in some groups, more aggressive behavior.

Pornographic has boost the sex industry which now generates $186 billion annually.[22]

What is clear is that the sex industry has become increasingly demanding of actors, actresses, performers, and users. Producers have also developed techniques aimed at drawing young people into the industry through what is now referred to as 'sexual grooming.' "About 63% of sex trafficking victims are women, while 37% are girls."[23]

Sexual Grooming

Many countries have enacted laws specifically targeting 'sexual grooming.' The routine that we are about to describe is used by criminals or sexual offenders to profit from or contribute to the sex industry. This is especially alarming because of the growing needs of an oversexualized world. To date, many adults remain unaware of the dangers that sexual grooming poses to their families and loved ones. This, by comparison, is what an overcharged sexual environment replicates to lead us to pornography.

The first step is 'befriending' the target. Abusers—in the worst case, recruiters—can be found everywhere in cafes, professional or social parties, schools or universities, and even among officemates or the participants of church gatherings. We all appreciate the company of friendly people, and this is the way they come into our circle. We usually have a guarded reaction when someone approaches us for the first time but after a short, open-minded, and friendly conversation, we postpone judgment, trusting in a self-developed confidence—often without much foundation.

The next stage is 'acquaintanceship.' Our new pal—usually good-looking and attractive—keeps in contact and little by little 'opens' our mind to a new set of rules, which we knew were there but dared never to challenge.

Fig. 8. The first step is 'befriending' the target.

The new acquaintance seems interested in everything we do, and our trust increases. Our new companion leads us to other friendly people who introduce us to smoking, alcohol, soft drugs—and even soft pornography. This new group of people isolates us from those who could help, discarding the values that we had as old-fashioned and outdated.

The third and last stage is 'capitalizing.' Once our values are replaced by anti-values, our new confidant can do anything with us. When this happens, the exploiter can confidently overstep the boundaries of friendship capitalizing on coercion, abuse, and blackmailing. The victims can do little about this last stage. It takes a lot of effort to get away from it; few are spared.

The Matrix

The same 'technology' is employed widely to turn as many people as possible into porn consumers and 'feed' the industry.

Fig. 9. Source: *Wired* — The instantly recognizable "digital rain" imagery from *The Matrix*.

In the movie *The Matrix*, humans serve as an energy source for the machines that have taken control of the world. After a war between humans and machines, the machines enslave humanity by plugging their bodies into a simulated reality (the Matrix), where humans live out their lives unaware of the truth.

While in the Matrix, humans' bodies generate bioelectric energy, which the machines harvest to sustain themselves. In this dystopian reality, humans are essentially "batteries" for machines, their minds trapped in a digital illusion.[24]

The new Matrix of today is the porn industry that through illusion brings people to feed the machinery that has generated the most profitable business in the world.

The first step in our transformation—'befriending'—is initiated by the so-called 'soft pornography' or sexually suggestive materials. Soft pornography relies more on allusion, innuendo, and sensual imagery. This type of content is often found in films, magazines, or television to create an erotic atmosphere without crossing into explicit sexual material.

Examples include suggestive scenes in movies, sensual content in popular songs, lingerie modeling, evocative art forms, and online lifestyle content. You find links to sex-oriented pages on the healthiest websites, unwanted pop-ups, or floating windows that lead you to sensual content in videos, news, and articles almost everywhere on the net. And if you browse for toys on most e-commerce or online retail platforms, your search results may include items like men's and women's underwear, playful innuendos, and even Viagra.

People feel very confident about their capacity to control urges. We might think that peeping short over a restricted website would not affect us at all because we are grown-up adults. Contrary to what we thought, our immaturity leads us to satisfy our curiosity. This step stages the second level in sexual grooming: acquaintanceship.

Little by little, we grow in the habit of visiting soft-pornography sites because, we believe, they are harmless. The urges to shift our online searches from soft porn to more explicit graphic materials goad us every time we return home from work.

Eventually, we give in with the conviction that we can cut short this habit anytime we want. Unsuspectedly, a new world of pleasure appears in front of us. A new land in need of discovery offers the help we need to rest from the difficulties that we experience every day. We are now stepping on the last stage of the grooming process: capitalization.

From now on, the way is open to all porn extremes. We spend more and more time searching for new graphic materials and explicit videos. We pay for subscriptions, explore new genders, and start losing contact with a meaningless reality around us and the people we should be caring for. We are now hooked.

The Brain

Regular porn consumers—Gary Wilson tells us in his book *Your Brain on Porn*—trigger plastic changes in their brain maps. The quest for exciting content evolves too. The constant search for new porn, themes, and stories on the Web alters their brain even without them realizing it.

Fig. 10. **Gary Bruce Wilson** (1956 – 2021) was an American writer and anti-pornography campaigner.

When something new grabs your attention, your brain basically makes room for it and lets the old stuff fade into the background.

One of the more striking effects is the detection of a decrease in the frontal gray matter of the brain. Fewer nerve connections here translate into sluggish activity and responses.

"In May 2014, the prestigious medical journal JAMA Psychiatry published research showing that, even in moderate porn users, use (number of years and current hours per week) correlates with reduced grey matter and decreased sexual responsiveness."[25]

A reduction of gray matter leads to impulsive and poor decision-making so much needed in executive functions like planning, reasoning, and self-control.[26] Individuals may experience mood swings, increased aggression, and a lack of awareness of inappropriate behavior. They can even detect a decline in cognitive abilities, including attention span, memory, and the processing of information. Loss of gray matter can also result in additional cravings that are now more difficult to resist.[27]

Drinking clear, crystalline water from a natural spring in the mountains is one of the simpler pleasures of the mountaineer. If the water is contaminated, his or her pleasure turns into a nightmare: what appears to be natural has shown itself to conflict with nature. We can think of porn as drinking poisonous water or as a toxic substance that contaminates our minds. Here, the eyes serve as the entry point for this corruption which affects our neural systems profoundly.

"The central nexus of this reward circuitry," Neuroscientists explain, "is a set of subcortical structures that lie just above and behind the eyes.

These structures are usually referred to collectively as the ventral striatum."[28]

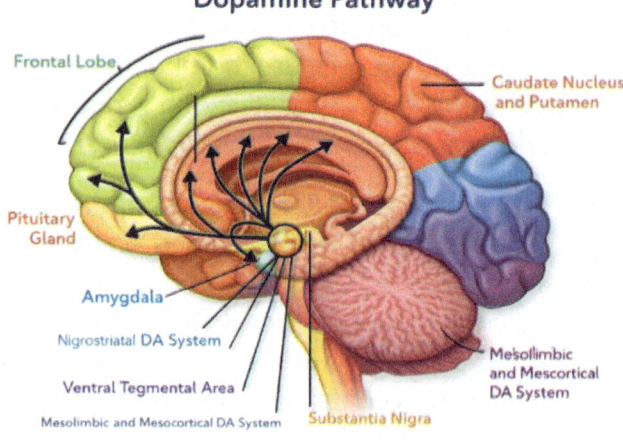

Fig. 11. Dopamine is a neurotransmitter that acts as a critical trigger for the release of hormones that regulate sexual activity and other pleasurable behaviors.

The ventral striatum is a complex brain region responsible for motivating us to seek out and engage in pleasurable activities. It plays a vital role in dopamine production and the regulation of our behavior.

Dopamine is a neurotransmitter that acts as a critical trigger for the release of certain hormones that regulate sexual activity and other pleasurable behaviors.

It works in concert with hormones like testosterone, estrogen, and oxytocin to regulate the overall sexual experience.

Dopamine stimulates areas of the brain like the hypothalamus and pituitary gland that signal the testes (in males) and ovaries (in females) to produce testosterone which boosts sexual desire. In females, dopamine indirectly affects estrogen production too enhancing sexual receptivity and desire.

At first, viewing porn is registered by the brain as satisfying. "But if you chronically overstimulate yourself, your brain may start to work against you. It protects itself against excessive dopamine by decreasing its responsiveness to it, and you feel less and less gratified. This decreased sensitivity to dopamine pushes some users into an even more determined search for stimulation, which, in turn, drives lasting changes, and actual physical alterations of the brain. They can be challenging to reverse."[29]

Addiction brings the user to search for what is called *supernova stimulation* driving him or her to unimaginable extremes never thought possible.

Pornographic addiction is real. "I think [ours is] a study that can help people understand that this is a real pathology, this is a real disorder, so people will not dismiss compulsive sexual behavior as something moralistic. ... This is not different from how pathologic gambling and substance addiction were viewed several years ago."[30]

Even if you are not an addict you are still at risk. We are vulnerable because the environment leads to addiction.

The Drug

Several studies are being conducted on the usage and effect of pornography in men and women. The consensus compares it to the introduction of tobacco and smoking. Consumers initially defended smoking as harmless, though they acknowledged some negative effects. Eventually, studies revealed the truth, leading to a decline in the tobacco industry and transforming smoking into a recognized voluntary harm.

Pornography can be compared to a drug. There are many websites—and even radio programs in some countries—dedicated to people who want to get away from pornography. There is an abundance of testimonials regarding the harmful effects of pornography and the recovery journeys of many individuals.

While most porn users are male, women favor it too. "One study found that 76% of females between the ages of 18 and 30 years old watch pornographic material. The number decreases as women age, with only 16% of females watching porn by the age of 50. Additionally, 55% of married males reported viewing porn as opposed to only 25% of married females."[31]

Because men are generally more visual than women, it's more common for women seeking pornography to spend time engaging with *erotica* and fantasizing about it. "There are entire forums dedicated to the type of erotica you want."[32]

Withdrawal and Detox

Withdrawal might be compared to smoking or drugs depending on the level of addiction and the resolve of the person. A person addicted to smoking might not find quitting particularly challenging.

However, withdrawing from pornography could lead some individuals to experience symptoms similar to those associated with drug addiction: "insomnia, anxiety, irritability, mood swings, headaches, restlessness, fatigue, poor concentration, depression, social paralysis, and cravings. Some also report more startling symptoms, such as shaking, flu-like symptoms, muscle cramps, or the mysterious sudden loss of libido that guys call the flatline."

"My symptoms after quitting: extreme exhaustion, restless sleep, muscle aches, joint pains and fever, mild disorientation, tension in the chest/tight breathing and anxiousness."[33]

The recovery process is possible but slow and demands patience. It begins in the mind through understanding and is achieved through abstinence, and avoiding triggers.

Triggers are situational, reminding us of the moments and circumstances that led to an urge to watch pornography—whether it's specific furniture, environments, or other cues. It's important to identify and avoid these reminders.

First, we need reasons. If we are not convinced of the destructive power of pornography, we will never step out of it.

These pages are supposed to help you reach that conclusion and lead you to a better understanding of sexuality.

Our sexuality is a gift that should be cared for and protected. It is the power within us manifesting itself in the welfare of family and society. It is the foundation of a serene and meaningful life.

Chapter Three: It's Complicated

What does truly define a homosexual? "Homosexuality is sexual attraction, romantic attraction, or sexual behavior between members of the same sex or gender."[34]

Effeminate or tomboyish stereotypes—using the most common language in our society—along with differences in preferences, tastes, personal likes and dislikes, upbringing, or even strong bonds of affection between close friends do not define someone as homosexual. Only sexual behavior does.

Homosexuals experience a desire for romantic relationships and sexual intimacy with people of the same sex, but friends—and many other individuals who are labeled as gay—do not. Friendship is characterized by a deep bond of affection, trust, and support between individuals, without romantic or sexual attraction.

On the other hand, particular circumstances may involuntarily lead a person to adopt mannerisms typically associated with the opposite sex. Let me emphasize that these are not manifestations of homosexuality.

For example, factors such as one's education or treatment at home — including relationship styles with parents, emotional indifference, overprotectiveness, absence of parental figures, insecurity, or excessive pressure regarding school performance — can lead to confusion about gender expression or preferences.

Another common ground of confusion is in specific personality profile. These special personality profiles could show in a lack of confidence in oneself, emotivity and a physical need for affection, attachments to people, and the lack of self-control.

Fig. 12. Perhaps you've never thought of it that way — can we call it a game, artificial, constructed for the benefit of its players?

Artists might misunderstand feelings of attraction towards people of the same sex as homosexual, without realizing that it is just their penchant for beauty.

However, many questions remain unanswered. What is going on? Who is behind these campaigns to promote homosexuality? What facts are we overlooking? Is our perception being carefully shaped?

In moments like these, it's easy to disengage—to avoid questioning and to steer clear of controversy. Controversy is expected, especially from a wealthy and influential minority determined to defend their slogans and outcries. Yet what we need is understanding, compelling arguments, and, above all, the truth.

We need answers because confused victims—many of them young adults and children—struggle with questions about their identity, their integrity, and their future. It is these individuals, the ones caught in confusion, whom I hope will find clarity and inspiration throughout the pages of this book.

Constructivism and Postmodernism

Today hyper-eroticism, hedonism, relativism, or gender ideology may encourage promiscuity and even outright homosexuality too, simply because such behaviors are made to seem fashionable—almost like a game.

Perhaps you've never thought of it that way — can we call it a game? A game is something artificial, something constructed for the benefit of its players.

Circumstances and causes behind misunderstanding will be treated later in this chapter, but for now we need to trace the present ideological roots that few people are able to identify.

38—It's Complicated

History tells us that Alexander the Great and Julius Caesar were both sexually fluid—men, soldiers, and conquerors. However, they did not advocate for gay rights or seek special inclusions.

Many people look to the cultural circumstances of the past to justify the current campaigns of LGBTQ+ lobby groups, when figures like Alexander the Great, Julius Caesar, and others couldn't have cared less.

Fig. 13. **Caesar** in the Vatican Museum, and the Mosaic of **Alexander** in the House of Fauno, Pompey
(Public Domain, Wikimedia Commons).

What we are experiencing today is simply the practical expression of so-called constructivism and postmodernism, both of which are rooted in Marxist ideology. And yes, even though Marxism may seem to have left center stage in many ways, it has evolved into other purely materialistic forms.[35]

Constructivism defends the view that knowledge is actively constructed by individuals rather than passively received from the external world.[36] Postmodernism promotes skepticism about reason, objectivity, progress, and universal truths, favoring pluralism and subjectivity. Both lead to relativism.

You've probably heard of the queer theory. It's widely promoted today, but it is essentially a byproduct of constructivism and the broader Woke movement.

Fig. 14. **Judith Butler and Michel Foucault**.
The main architects of the Queer Theory
(licensed under CC BY 2.0, via Wikimedia Commons).

The queer theory challenges the belief that gender and sexuality are fixed, binary categories. Because it lacks a biological foundation, it encourages the idea that our feelings, thoughts, and beliefs can define our reality. As a result, some individuals attempt to conform to their perceived reality through surgical procedures that lead to gender transitions.

However, queer theory—and, more broadly, gender ideology—raises a difficult and controversial issue: 'disassociation from reality.' Many supporters overlook the fact that dissociation from reality is a mental health condition with serious consequences.

Disassociation from Reality

In psychiatry, mental health conditions that involve a break from reality—such as delusions or detachment—are known as psychotic disorders.

Fig. 15. In psychiatry, mental health conditions that involve a break from reality are known as psychotic disorders.

The ideological basis of some current cultural trends reflects similar patterns of disconnection.

Sexuality in Overdrive?—41

For example, schizophrenia—characterized by disorganized thinking and false beliefs—and schizoaffective disorder—which combines symptoms of psychosis with mood disturbances—are clinical examples of how severe detachment from reality can manifest.

Fig. 16. **Irving Bieber** (1909-1991) and **Charles Socarides** (1922-2005) co-founders of the National Association for Research & Therapy of Homosexuality
(Scanned from the cover of one of his books.
Used under fair use. Via Wikimedia Commons).

Until 1973, homosexuality was classified as a mental disorder in the Diagnostic and Statistical Manual of Mental Disorders (DSM) by the American Psychiatric Association (APA). This classification was challenged by activists and researchers, notably Dr. Evelyn Hooker, whose 1950s studies showed no difference in mental health between homosexual and heterosexual men.

In 1973, the APA voted to remove homosexuality from the DSM though a residual category called "sexual orientation disturbance" remained until 1987.[37]

It is difficult to gain a clear perspective on what truly happened in 1973. A lot has changed since then, and today many specialists argue that what queer theory and contemporary gender ideologies promote aligns with what psychologists and psychiatrists fear most.

Well-known psychiatrists like Dr. Irving Bieber[38] and Dr. Charles Socarides[39] have challenged this decision and founded the National Association for Research and Therapy of Homosexuality (NARTH). He has published extensively on the controversy,[40] promoting reparative therapy. He has been widely criticized and marginalized for his views.

Consider this a warning to those who embrace constructivist and postmodern theories: dissociation from reality is a serious condition. Those who suffer from it eventually become impaired— unable to relate to others, emotionally unstable, and trapped in a psychosis where they believe they are isolated and constantly misunderstood for who they perceive themselves to be.

Let us encourage those who feel outcast or rejected because of their homosexuality seek their true identity and explore how their physical makeup as men and women aligns with their nature—instead of distancing themselves from it: the search for a fictitious reality can lead to despair. Life is greater than sexual desire.

The Scientific Claims

The current cultural push toward a homosexual lifestyle can be seen as artificial, especially if it lacks a biological foundation. After all, there is no known "homosexual chromosome" or consistent, viable genetic mutation linked to it.[41]

The Homosexual Chromosome

The biggest research ever done on the subject and published in the prestigious *Science*, *Harvard Magazine* tells that "There is no one gene for being gay, and though genes seem to play a role in determining sexual orientation and same-sex behavior, it's small, complex, and anything but deterministic. That's the conclusion of a paper by an international team of researchers, co-led by Benjamin Neale of the Broad Institute of Harvard and MIT, published today in the journal Science. (The team combed the genomes of more than 470,000 people in the United States and the United Kingdom to see how genetic variants at millions of different places in the genome correlate with whether participants had ever had sex with someone of the same sex.)"[42]

Honest, serious researchers—though many raise concerns about their underlying motivations—continue to tell us: "There may be a biological foundation, but as of now, we cannot prove it."

44—It's Complicated

What we do find, however, are various contributing factors: hormonal imbalances and mental health disorders; the harmful effects of public policy; the widespread presence of estrogens in commercially available products; sex addiction and drug use; and cultural elements such as ignorance, upbringing, and social pressure.

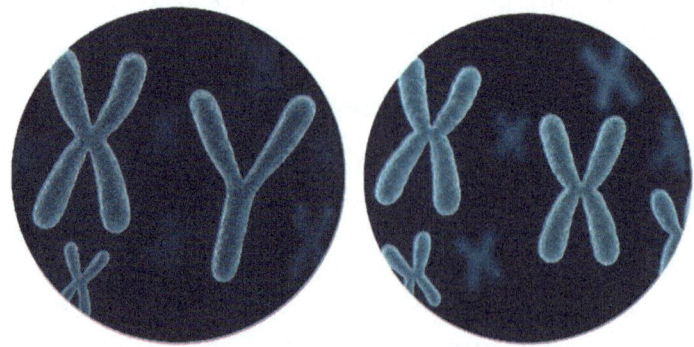

Fig. 17. XY for male and XX for female are the standard biological representation for sex chromosomes in humans.

Gender ideologists and supporters justify their opinions by saying that external factors and mutations interfere with the development of the endocrine system becoming agents of sexual change. Is this opinion supported by the scientific world?

External Agents

Huberman in his Lab Podcast explains that certain external agents infiltrating the city's water supply can alter the chemical composition of what we drink and cause hormonal imbalance. He also explains that cosmetics and commercially available drugs could impact the development of sexual organs in children, particularly during pregnancy, as well as influence the sexual preferences of individuals.[43]

The two main classes of sex hormones are androgens and estrogens, of which the most important human derivatives are testosterone and estradiol, respectively. In general, androgens are considered male sex hormones, since they have masculinizing effects, while estrogens and progestogens are considered female sex hormones although all types are present in each sex at different levels.

Examples of these external agents are primeval oils, the estrogenic effects of herbicides that affect the development of testis; the consumption of Cannabis, marihuana, which increases testosterone activity; the effect of alcohol that increases estrogenic activity; the popularity of sport hormones and some sports supplements that change the level of testosterone and enhance physical activity.

Huberman's arguments are vague. Generally, the effects of hormonal imbalance are reversible, except for exposure during fetal development, which can result in irreversible changes—to reproductive organs or brain development. He claims that the complexity of the endocrine system might develop perfectly normal gender alternatives.[44] He goes to the extent of recommending hormonal treatment to enhance any given sexual choice—and so acknowledge that treatment can reverse homosexual inclinations if wanted.

This is rather confusing because prestigious studies by Swift-Gallant, et al., examining hormonal influences by hormonal irregularities—even when caused by external agents—do not reliably "change" a person's sexual orientation.[45] Psychologists and psychiatrists have already proven that changes in sexual orientation are caused by cultural, not biological factors.

But how about mutations?

Mutations

Beyond these external factors influencing gender behavior—Huberman explains—we find genetic mutations that modify the natural development of the individual.

For example, the discovery in 1970 of a mutation in the Dominican Republic named Guevedoces, brings males to appear as females until puberty when the male genitalia develop.

Another mutation is Androgen Insensitivity Syndrome (AIS), a genetic condition in which a person who is genetically male (with one X and one Y chromosome) is partially or completely resistant to androgens— male sex hormones like testosterone. In Complete Androgen Insensitivity Syndrome (CAIS)— the hardcore manifestation of the syndrome— individuals are genetically male but appear physically female due to their body's inability to respond to androgens.

In both cases the appearance of these phenomena is rare[46] and the people suffering from this condition are not reproductively viable.

Lobbying Groups

No one can blame scientists for pushing hard to comply with the pressure imposed by committed groups around the world and avoid their influencing power.[47]

Fig. 18. Is the claim 'sexual orientation is not a choice' compatible with human freedom? If not, what does the slogan 'right to choose' mean?

These groups need money to gain legislation and justify their presence. And they can generate lots of funds from many organizations, grants, funding events, foundations, advocacy networks, individual donations, corporate sponsorships, and through private channels or undisclosed sources.

Their campaigns often lead the disoriented, doubtful, and misguided unwittingly to their ranks because of misinformation.

A lot of misguiding has been done through a delusion of psychological factors that lead to homosexuality.

Today, LGBTQ+ groups, the American Psychological Organization, and the World Health Organization support that *sexual orientation is not a choice* but a complex interplay of biological, psychological, and environmental factors.

They argue that a person who feels like a homosexual—or who is labeled as one—is, in fact, a homosexual. To imply that any form of homosexuality is 'not a choice' is to misinform people.

Discussions on this matter will continue indefinitely, because the influence, money, and power of these lobbying groups will always find ways to counter scientific facts to support an opinion that today lacks a solid foundation.

Abuse

Mental, physical, and environmental factors can wear down a person's natural responses—we are not referring here to congenital, hereditary, or hormonal imbalances. When this happens, some people's feelings—without generalizing—may come under pressure, turning inward toward a self-centered and self-motivated search for sexual pleasure. The most honest word for these consummated pleasures is "abuse" or "self-abuse." But to grasp how serious abuse is, we need to examine what it does to the person.

Abuse, in general, comes in many forms and shapes. It was even justified by famous scientists like Alfred Kinsey who defended that 'There is no normality and no abnormality.'

The cycles of abuse are terrifying and multiply exponentially. When depraved, the abused may eventually become the abuser.

Pedophilia, perversion, sexual fetishism, harassment, rape, promiscuity, queer behavior, disregard for life, bizarre sexual practices, and sexual violence often contribute to abuse or spring from it. The rise of new venereal diseases, suicidal behavior, depression, drug abuse, loneliness, and social isolation indicates that something is deeply wrong.

We'll begin with self-abuse—rather internal—before we look at the different kinds of external abuse.

Pornography

Testimonies collected by Gary Wilson in his book *Your Brain on Porn* show that cycles of self-abuse lead some users to homosexuality.

"(Age 19) I seriously thought I was turning gay. My HOCD [Homosexual Obsessive-Compulsive Disorder] was so strong at that time, that I was contemplating diving the nearest high-rise. I felt so depressed. I knew I loved girls, and I couldn't love another dude, but why did I have ED [Erection

Disorder]? Why did I need transgender/gay stuff to shock me into arousal?"[48]

"I had HOCD, in the sense that I feared myself to actually be heterosexual since I eventually was exclusively turned on by straight and 'lesbian' porn. Yes, 'feared,' because my entire social identity was as a gay man, and I am married to a man. If I went 'back to straight' – a move that nobody would ever believe and is more taboo nowadays than coming out as gay – I would be a social outcast."[49]

Porn users in general detect in themselves a gradual dialing down of a person's sensitivity to all pleasure even in moderate porn users[50]—explained in the section 'The brain' in the previous chapter. Desensitization leads them to look for more self-satisfying experiences, creating a dependency, an addiction, in the process.

What pornography promotes is a habit that does not simply gratify desire through self-abuse but gradually trains it — often in directions the user never intended.

Traumatic Sexual Experiences

Psychosexual maturity is parallel to the development of traumatic sexual experiences and emotional wounds. In this new case, we are talking about the way victims of various ages are damaged by touch or violence to the point of misunderstanding their sexuality.

This is one of the more difficult, controversial, and heartbreaking cases of abuse which affects the psyche of the victim to the extent of disorienting his or her emotions and behavior.

Childhood sexual abuse has profound and long-lasting effects on its victims like Post-Traumatic Stress Disorder which includes symptoms like flashbacks, severe anxiety, and uncontrollable thoughts about the experienced abuse; depression which can persist into adulthood; low self-esteem; behavioral issues at school; emotional and social impact; and even physical health-related problems.[51]

Fig. 19. Trafficking persists through global hubs, even though it is infrequent in international airports.

Statistics reflect cases of abuse in public establishments or by perverts, but often the more traumatic experiences come from close relatives, people employed at home, friends, or neighbors.

When abuse happens at home at the hands of someone of the same sex, children often feel emotions they later misinterpret as homosexual—feelings they usually keep to themselves until much later, if they ever find someone they trust enough to talk to.[52]

Globally, it is estimated that 1 in 4 girls and 1 in 6 boys experience sexual abuse before the age of 18. Approximately 89% of the victims are female, while 11% are male.[53]

Cultural Factors

We all grow up in cultural environments that shape much of what we understand about ourselves, our families, society, and the world at large. Ideas about right and wrong blend into complex patterns of behavior, usually tied to the historical moment we're living in.

This is why it's not surprising to find people who are completely disoriented, people who, in many cases, couldn't have known any better.

These next pages are dedicated to them. It isn't easy to sort out the positive and the negative in the environment we grew up in, or in the ways we've developed.

School Regulations

It is increasingly difficult to be a father or a mother in a world where totalitarian ideas—yes, let's face it—are broadcasted by state regulations regarding sex education in private and public schools.

Official statistics on sex education[54] show a contradictory sexual anarchy reflecting the chaos paraded by most of the official programs.

Fig. 20. Children are the responsibility of their parents not of the state.

Many of today's most popular public sex-education programs teach and promote early sexual intercourse, undermine parental authority through persuasive messaging, introduce children to confusing gender-ideology slogans and choices. This, too, can be seen as a form of child abuse carried out by legislators who claim to know better than parents.

Much of this traces back to political ideologies and the agendas of lobbying groups—for example, the roughly 30 new LGBTQ-related education laws that went into effect in 2023 as students returned to school across the United States.⁵⁵

We all must grow into men and women; this is part of human nature. Here is where the difficult journey begins.

Fig. 21. There is no single global count, but in most countries homeschooling represents under 5% of school-age children.

Children are the responsibility of their parents not of the state. If the state believes that parents lack the necessary training or interest, it could offer programs to assist them, not to replace them—which was and still is the totalitarian style in countries notorious for their ruthless approach to education.

Fortunately, several initiatives have been launched to raise parents' awareness of their responsibilities and encourage greater involvement in their children's education. We find them in the United States (Parents for Healthy Schools), UNESCO's Parental Support Programs, the United Kingdom (Parentkind), Australia (Learning Potential Resources), Canada (Parents as Partners), and the Philippines (Parent Effectiveness Service Program Act—Republican Act 11908[56]).

Many parents are now turning to homeschooling as an alternative to both public and private education, especially in places where other options aren't available.

Home and the Environment

The roles of both father and mother are essential for those who don't just want what's good, but what's best for their children. "A father should feel the challenge of being a father to his son or daughter. The same applies to mothers, though what each is challenged to is different according to his or her proper sexual role."[57]

The challenge is, at times, underestimated. Inadvertently, the mother who wanted a girl but got a boy would favor a girly treatment that might turn her boy into an effeminate. While the father who wanted a boy but got a girl could turn her into a tomboy. This could happen in the case of absent parents too.

Other styles of relationship between parents and children might also end up complicating matters like overprotective parents who make the children soft and vulnerable; the parents' indifference to the insecure or extreme emotional drive of their children; performance-driven demands lacking the affective support of parents; fights between parents, and the absence of affection towards their children.

It is well-known the advice of Jason Evert who shared many insights on sexual education, among them the relationship father-daughter: "Fathers, embrace your daughters. Let them know what a man's love means, so they don't go looking for it in the wrong places [i.e., lesbian love]."

Children and young adults who exhibit tastes and mannerisms typically associated with the opposite sex often encounter teasing and bullying from teachers, classmates, neighbors, and even friends.

The misunderstood are often labeled as homosexual and treated that way—even when they're not—but people's attitudes can wear them down and push them to look for support outside their usual circles.

If you add pornography, hyper-eroticized media, cultural hedonism, sexual permissiveness, and constant gender-related demands promoted by pressure groups, you risk turning those who are misunderstood into victims—already confused and with almost no chance of finding clarity.

The solution might be tough but simpler. First, let them feel your understanding and affection. Then, avoid leaving them in the hands of people who don't have any educational role in your family. Your child might need a change of school or neighborhood too. And let them discover that the proper habits and values corresponding to their sex and age are worth pursuing and rewarding in many ways.

If you are the victim, keep an open mind, don't believe whatever they tell you about your homosexual tendencies—even if you have indulged in sexual practices—and seek advice. You can find people—through social media or private organizations—who can help you recover what you thought was lost. You might also need a change of environment and friends, and, maybe, even a new job.

Personality Profiles

A personality profile is used to describe an individual's characteristic reasoning patterns, feelings, and behaviors. The components of a personality profile include traits, strengths and weaknesses, motivation, tendencies, emotional responses, and personal skills.

Appreciation of beauty is a key trait that defines a unique type of personality profile, especially important in the arts. It is common to find artists like musicians, painters, designers, net artists, writers, architects, and many others whose job is to showcase beauty. It is also common among them to find people who declare themselves homosexual. Why so?

Beauty is captivating in whatever form it is represented and brings with it the desire to possess it, a desire that demands control and moderation.

Perhaps the best-known artists celebrated for their sculpture are Gian Lorenzo Bernini and Michelangelo di Lodovico Buonarroti Simoni.

Fig. 22 **Apollo and Daphne**
(exhibited in the Galleria Borghese
(Villa Borghese), in Rome).

Bernini's work, *Apollo and Daphne* among others, shows how the human form can take shape in beauty without reducing it to mere sensuality. The sculpture is exhibited in the Galleria Borghese (Villa Borghese), in Rome, where it has been housed since 1625.

"*Apollo and Daphne* are often considered Bernini's most miraculous work. The moment Daphne transforms into a tree [after Apollo's touch]— bark climbing her torso, leaves bursting from her fingers — is carved with such delicacy that it feels impossible. It's a sculpture that captures motion, emotion, and myth all at once."[58]

Bernini's masterpiece tells us more through the story of *Apollo and Daphne*. When beauty is violated by a possessive, unlawful desire, it turns into a shapeless form, meaningless to the touch, lacking appeal and grace.

Appreciation of beauty can lead to confusion. The confusion arises from a recognition of beauty in both males and females equally. This appreciation for same-sex forms of expression is not synonymous with homosexuality but far from it.

This, along with other factors such as the emotional intensity of friendship, care, and attention, may lead some individuals to perceive themselves as homosexual. Additionally, the aggressive sexual values found in social environments can contribute to this perception.

Surely, confusion is also present in the minds of another type of personality profile that promotes nudism and naturism arising from a meaningless approach to sexuality and a kind of sexual indifferentism. It is difficult to judge their attitude, which seems to proceed from ignorance and, perhaps, from a sensual approach to life that, eventually, brought about a senseless view of sexuality.

At any rate, anyone searching for light and for a clearer understanding of what an apparent homosexual or senseless desire might mean can find real help through the right person, the right advice, and honest reflection.

When individuals genuinely desire to make a change, reversing circumstances is always possible. This ability to adapt and grow highlights the power of human will and determination. Whether it's a shift in behavior, mindset, or circumstances, the decision to initiate change can pave the way for personal transformation. A renewed sense of purpose leads to profound and positive outcomes in one's life.

Chapter Four: Intimacy's Hack

Parties are so common today that few people question their nature or purpose. At one of these gatherings, after drinking too much, physical and sensual desires can grow irresistibly—whether toward your partner, the guest who invited you, or a new acquaintance. With mutual agreement, you may look for a quiet corner to "let off steam."

In such situations, the man may push forward with his desires, while the woman may initially give in but later try to stop, realizing that things have gone too far. When a man continues despite her resistance, the encounter can easily end at the police station with charges of rape.

This scenario is not fiction. Police stations and courts of justice—confirmed to me by a judge friend—are crowded with such cases. Both the victim and the abuser suffer a kind of violation: a violation of their own human nature, crossing boundaries they were never meant to cross.

We are learning more about the catastrophic effects of overdriven sexuality, which increasingly resembles a kind of pandemic. This new pandemic feeds on selfishness, misinformation, and ignorance, promoting false values that have become a curse upon humanity.

62—Intimacy's Hack

Sexually transmitted infections, venereal diseases, traumatic experiences, mental disorders, suicidal tendencies, existential emptiness, and even death appear to be the ultimate consequences of today's sexual frenzy.

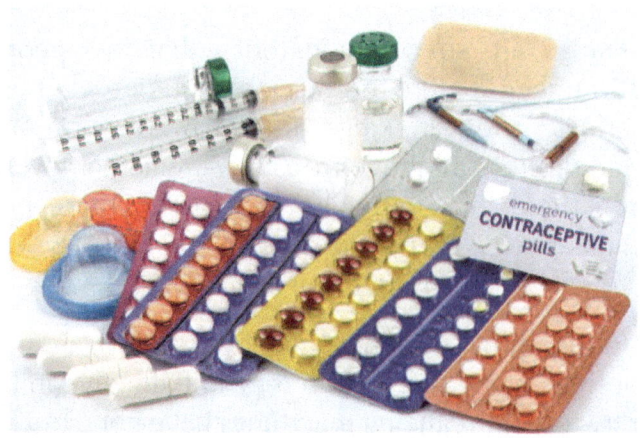

Fig. 23. Most common types of contraceptives: birth control pills, hormonal IUD, implant, hormonal injection, hormonal patch, condoms, diaphragm, cervical cap.

The question remains: who is promoting and supporting these campaigns? It is difficult to identify specific groups—some may operate in the background, almost like secret societies. But it is far easier to identify those who benefit from the situation: the companies that profit enormously from contraceptives.

The Contraceptive Mentality

When sexuality is reduced to the pursuit of pleasure alone, a contraceptive mentality naturally follows. Once pleasure becomes the primary goal, fertility is no longer seen as a gift but as an obstacle to manage or avoid.

This mentality gradually shapes the way people view pregnancy itself. What was once understood as the natural fruit of love is now treated almost like a disease—something to be prevented, controlled, or eliminated.

Pharmaceutical companies reinforce this shift through slogans that emphasize safety, empowerment, and worry-free relationships. Their campaigns move beyond simple birth control and promote a lifestyle of "safe sex," especially targeting the youth. The message is clear: pleasure without consequence. Let me give you some examples:

"Safe love is the best love"

"Love responsibly—gear up first!"

"Trust the latex, not your luck!"

"Safety is sexy—stay wrapped!"

"Love smart, love safe!"

"Confidence comes with protection!"

"Make love, not mistakes!"

"Your best accessory? A condom in your pocket!"

"Trust Trojan for a night to remember, not regret."

"Durex: Whatever is On Your Mind" (Clever Condoms)

"Thanks birth control" (Campaign by The National Campaign to Prevent Teen and Unplanned Pregnancy)

"Back off baby, I'm in school" (Targeting college students)

Yet the data available online shows that "safe" is not always safe. The consequences of these campaigns are visible in rising abortion numbers, the spread of sexually transmitted infections, and the emergence of sexual behaviors that harm individuals, families, and society at large.

Venereal diseases	STIs
Syphilis	Chlamydia trachomatis
Gonorrhoea	Mycoplasma genitalium
Chancroid	Mycoplasma hominis
Lymphogranuloma venereum	Ureoplasma urealyticum
Granuloma inguinale	Anaerobic bacteria
	Trichomonas vaginalis (TV)
	Candidiasis
	Pediculosis pubis
	Scabies
	Human immunodeficiency virus (HIV)
	Herpes simplex virus (HSV)
	Human papilloma virus (HPV)
	Hepatitis B virus (HBV)
	Ebola virus

The World Health Organization reports that approximately 73 million induced abortions occur worldwide each year. Studies consistently show that casual sexual relationships—especially those involving multiple partners—significantly increase the risk of STI transmission.

Sexuality in Overdrive?—65

Sexually transmitted disease	Patients No. of positive result/negative result (%)
Hepatitis B	5/281 (1.7/96.6)
Syphilis (VDRL positive)	2/284 (0.7/97.6)
AIDS (Anti-HIV positive)	0/286 (0/98.3)
Chlamydial infection	69/202 (23.7/69.4)
Gonorrhea	17/254 (5.8/87.3)
Trichomonas	6/263 (2.1/90.4)
Bacterial Vaginosis	174/98 (59.8/33.7)

VDRL, Venereal Disease Research Laboratory; AIDS, acquired immune deficiency syndrome; HIV, human immunodeficiency virus.

Fig. 24. A study of sexual assault: Based on data from Boramae One-stop Service Center (researchgate.net).

Fig. 25. Seoul Boramae Hospital.

A study of 291 sexual assault cases in Boramae Hospital (Seoul) reveals another troubling pattern: half of the abusers were acquaintances, friends, or partners, and half of the assaults occurred at home. The complications brought about by the assaults are shown in the table below.[59]

These patterns emerge in a cultural environment where premarital sex and live-in arrangements are increasingly normalized, often influenced by fears of marriage failure witnessed in one's own family.

Are you surprised? How have we all arrived at this point? We cannot simply blame pharmaceutical companies for the present state of affairs; we, too, have played our part. We soothe our conscience with justifications and excuses.

Today, most commonly, people appeal to "mother nature." We tell ourselves that our desires are natural because, after all, we are "just another animal," the accidental product of an evolutionary process that happened to place us at the top of the food chain.

But this view is incomplete. As stated earlier, we are not merely animals. Our reflective capacity, our cultural life, and our ethical and behavioral customs place us far above any other living creature. Something about us exceeds instinct.

Humans can step outside their own impulses, evaluate them, and freely choose to act against instinct for the sake of meaning, truth, or moral principle. No other animal demonstrates this level of reflective self-governance.

To understand this difference more deeply, it helps to turn to Aristotle, who was the first to propose a hierarchy of living beings based on the nature of their souls.

In his work *De Anima* ('On the Soul'), Aristotle defines the soul as: "The first actuality (*entelecheia*) of a natural body that has life potentially." The soul is the one that gives form to the matter.

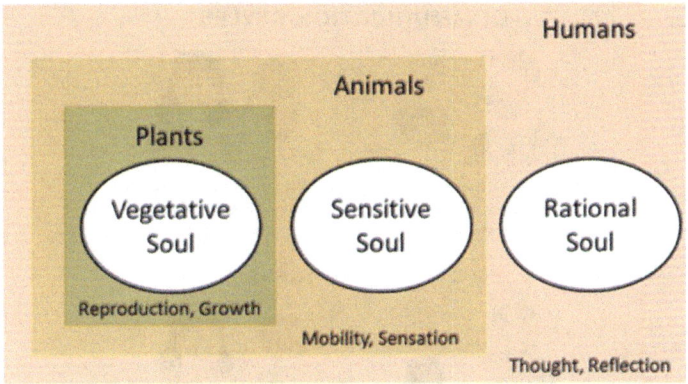

Fig. 26. The structure of the souls of plants, animals, and humans
(Ian Alexander, own work. Licensed under CC BY-SA 4.0. Via Wikimedia Commons).

Our soul —the Aristotelian soul— gives a specific human form to our sexuality, one fundamentally different from that of the animal kingdom. To become truly human, above every other living form, we must understand how this human soul "forms" our body, our desires, and our way of loving.

Exploring Stimuli and Desire

We can reach a deeper understanding of sexual behavior—and even the roots of promiscuity—by examining the real differences between men and women and the way they relate to one another. Men and women are not only physically distinct; they also tend to differ emotionally and psychologically.

> **FOOD FOR THOUGHT**
>
> ## MEN AND WOMEN ARE WIRED DIFFERENTLY
>
> **COMMUNICATION STYLES**
>
> Men often focus on facts, solutions, and outcomes.
>
> Women tend to focus on feelings, connection, and context.
>
> **EMOTIONAL PROCESSING**
>
> Men may internalize their emotions and process silently.
>
> Women often externalize emotions and need to talk through them.
>
> **Needs in Love**
> Men crave respect, honor, and appreciation.
> Women desire affection, security, and emotional presence.

Fig. 27. Source: Gary Deutschmann, via Facebook.

Men often approach life through responsibility, focus, and task-oriented action. Women, by contrast, tend to bring a relational and integrative dimension that humanizes and enriches society: their bodies and emotional constitution are naturally oriented toward nurturing life.

Men more commonly organize their experiences into compartments, while women weave them together into a unified whole

Similarly, we can talk about different stimuli and desire. When it comes to sexual attraction, women are more idealistic, conceptual; men are more direct and practical. Men are first and always visually attracted; women favor touch.

All senses play an important role in sexual attraction, but their impact can differ depending on the context and individual preferences. While there are some common seductive patterns between men and women —which, for example, explain the visual attraction towards pornographic materials—men might be more responsive to visual stimuli, while women might integrate a broader range of factors including touch, emotional, and social elements.[60]

This explains why women find no objection to their sexy looks: they are less visually motivated than men. A young customer in a nameless commercial center sported the following line printed on her shirt, 'The irresistible desire or being desired.' This is the bottom line of our discussion: do we want the desires of others? What type of desire do we want to awaken in others? What makes you desirable?

Women are more notional than men and often desire to shape a beautiful image of themselves welcoming with open arms whatever the latest fashion trends dictate. The exception is women engaging in the sex business and others who, knowingly, want to project a sexual image and indulge in the 'irresistible desire of being sexually desired.'

Fashionable women in sexy costumes might even call men 'perverts' after detecting questionable lewd glances. It is possible to find people under the category of perverts in the streets of our cities—perhaps more now than ever before—but often men just follow the pull of visual stimuli which for many is uncontrollable and justifiable. Is this good or bad? Do men and women need a command over their sexual appetites?

Sexy Looks

How sexy is sexy? One hundred and twenty years ago, a woman showing her ankle was sexy; you can easily see the contrast today.

Men and women of our time react differently to the display of skin.

Fashion has shortened the length of skirts, pants, and trousers year after year; shirts and blouses keep getting tighter, while many favor tights and jumpsuits both during and outside of exercise.

The name of the game is 'gain,' and you want to show it. You want others to see how much weight you've lost through diet; you want to display the muscles you've worked so hard to build; and that girl wants to parade her beautiful body, the envy of every girl in her school or workplace.

Teenage girls want to show that they are no longer children, that they are already women—their pride lies in their gain.

There may be many reasons to join a club and exercise intensely—health, confidence, rehabilitation, and more. Yet, without straying from our discussion, the way we present ourselves in public and the fashion we choose lead us to ask: How much of my body should I reveal? How much skin should I uncover? Does it matter if I wear clothing that enhances my well-shaped body?

Fig. 28. The name of the game is 'gain,' and you want to show it.

Do you favor very tight clothing which, as a friend of mine once said, 'leaves nothing to the imagination'? Even if you seem relaxed in the way you dress, I cannot judge you, because fashion has always influenced society and left an imprint on every era. Instead, I would like to encourage you to reflect on any possible desensitization in your manner of dress and in your values.

The person who exposes his or her sexuality with indifference loses part of own's intimacy. It is like an open faucet that drains away whatever it holds or preserves.

Little by little, exposing one's skin leads to more meaningless exposure—unless we recognize it as wrong. Sexual fantasies hold less appeal, and the indulging person looks for other avenues to express his or her desires. One's feelings are judged as normal, while the consternation in others is seen as abnormal.

Our sexuality is woven into our personality. When we lose its meaning, we lose part of ourselves as well. This loss of meaning is what fills nudist beaches: there is no longer any sense of relationship, and a kind of asexuality takes over. We see no other purpose in sexuality than parading our naked bodies in public.

Parading Intimacy

Most humans —we have explored some few exceptions— avoid parading their bodies naked. We give a lot of business to Louis Vuitton, Prada, Gucci, Versace, Burberry, and thousands of other fashion companies all over the world which tell you that nudity is not the human way.

Nobody knows—and will never know—what our distant ancestors wore. Yet pseudo-storyteller scientists insist on weaving accounts and spreading the idea that, being close to animals, we went around naked.

Sexuality in Overdrive?—73

Modern discoveries, however, seem to point in a different direction. Today, archaeologists are surprised to find that human remains dated thousands of years ago—yes, not just 40,000 years as with *Homo sapiens sapiens*—show striking similarities to modern features and customs.

Fig. 29. AI reconstruction of the Jebel man, based on the fossilized skull found at the site.

Excavations in 1960 at Jebel Irhoud, Morocco, during a mining operation, accidentally uncovered fossilized *Homo sapiens* remains. With newer dating methods, these remains revealed the impressive—and frankly surprising—age of 300,000 years.[61]

You might find this amusing, but one day at a hotel breakfast lounge I saw the Jebel man having coffee—it was the exact replica of the face created by imaging methods from the remains of the skull.

It is doubtful that *Homo sapiens* went around naked; many other artifacts and even paintings contradict that idea. And if they were naked, surely their intent would have been different from simply parading their sexuality.

Our interest in fashion—understood here as the need to cover our nakedness—not only motivates us to choose what we wear but also 'protects something of a personal, or private nature'—which is the definition that the Merriam-Western dictionary favors on 'intimacy' (other dictionaries define intimacy in the context of a 'sexual relationship').

Intimacy is a fundamental human right that takes many forms, much like a thesaurus filled with synonyms and antonyms. Concepts such as privacy, secrecy, respect, and identity are all connected to intimacy, with dignity playing a particularly important role.

When intimacy is publicly exposed, we lose not only our dignity but also the respect we deserve; we subject ourselves to public scrutiny and to the desires of those who have no right to interfere in our lives.

Today, reality shows on radio and TV, along with the press's assault on people's private lives, seem to justify the exposure of sexuality—as if the right to privacy did not exist.

Sexuality in Overdrive?—75

The reality show of primal survival *Naked and Afraid* drops contestants into remote, often harsh environments, where they must survive for 21 days with no clothing, no food, and no shelter. The show has been running for several seasons, and its popularity seems to stem from the sensual approach of the challenge. It has been a commercial success, combining nudity, isolation, extreme survival, high-stakes drama, and romance. However, the program is also facing strong opposition for the obvious anti-values portrait in the making.[62]

Fig. 30. The series premiered on the Discovery Channel on June 23, 2013. As of today, 2026, it is currently in its 19th season.

What values would the protagonist in the *Naked and Afraid* series hold? And what values does a person have who parades a sex appeal as bait to build a story? Sex is more than a commodity.

A Human Right

As a human right, any voluntary violation of sexual intimacy is punishable. Indecent exposure refers to the display of one's sexual organs in a public or non-consensual context. Such acts can be particularly distressing, especially to minors, and are often treated as criminal offenses.

Yet we encounter much of this intimate world in advertisements everywhere. By appearances, today's society has descended into a kind of indifferent sexual anarchy, showing little concern for escaping it.

The famous slogan 'No Gods, no Masters' has become a dominant cry. But what happens to a society left unprotected by law? We need guiding principles and sound directives: we need good principles and just laws.

Laws establish standards of behavior that help maintain order in society; without them, it is impossible for people to flourish. But laws must be grounded in human nature and reason; otherwise, they will prove ineffective.

Laws that regulate behavior are generally referred to as regulatory laws or behavioral laws. Such laws define what is right and what is wrong. Yet the most heated discussions among lawmakers often center on the foundation of these laws: What is ethically right, and what is ethically wrong?

Debates among politicians from different parties, each pushing their own agendas, raise tough questions about the very nature of our laws. Can lawmakers enact just laws rooted in a moral and ethical human order? In theory, yes. But in practice, it all comes down to the character of the legislators—their moral formation, their prudence, their integrity. And let's be honest, those qualities don't usually shine through election campaigns.

Fig. 31. Can a heated debate determine what is right or wrong?

Lawmakers have a better chance of passing laws aligned with the objective moral good—what classical philosophy calls natural law—when they advocate respect for human dignity, promote the common good, and protect fundamental rights.

Still, even with good intentions, it's hard to avoid laws that end up arbitrary or self-serving. Human nature is fragile, and the pressure from powerful lobbying groups can easily sway the process, bending it away from what's truly ethical and good for the people.

Endless controversies—often arising from confusion about principles and the application of the law—will likely continue rage forever.

Fig. 32. Is it possible for the influence of lobbyists to change the definition of right or wrong?

Because there are no perfect behavioral laws, or because these laws are deficient, we must deepen our understanding of the issues at play and embrace the principles of moral order. Learning enables us to recognize what the legislator overlooks—respect for human dignity, the promotion of the common good, and the protection of fundamental rights.

We can identify where intimacy is violated by understanding what human sexuality truly means. We should recognize that the true motivation behind sexuality is love and the heritage found in the fruits of that love.

True Love vs. Self-Love

Think about it: love is the ultimate reason. It's what moves people forward, helps them overcome difficulties, change direction, and find purpose and strength.

Fig. 33. What is love?

Love can take many forms. It may show itself in a project pursued with passion for the benefit of others, in the commitment of religious dedication, in caring for those who need us most—especially family bound by blood—and, ultimately, in the family itself.

Love is so essential—so ultimate—that without it, life makes no sense. To love and to be loved is truly the highest goal, the only one that leads us to real happiness—which, in the end, is what we are all searching for.

Yet there is a common form of love that eventually drags us down. We all share in it: self-love. Self-love leads nowhere. For love to be real, it requires two people.

Reciprocity means not only receiving love from the person we care for but also sharing in the joy, the good, and the happiness we wish for others. This is the condition of love we cannot escape.

Self-love is empty because our ego cannot love us back; we are only one person, not two. It leads only to a restless frenzy to satisfy our desires without ever finding true fulfillment.

This is the kind of love that interferes with every relationship: the search for oneself in the act of giving oneself. The person who looks only for himself or herself in a relationship will always feel unsatisfied.

Even with a partner, the indifference in how one gives oneself becomes clear. No matter what you say or the feelings you awaken in your partner, the pursuit is solely for pleasure. In short, you are still searching for yourself.

This makes the relationship unstable, often leading to extremes—boredom, indifference, and eventually the search for someone who mirrors your own desires.

Some forms of homosexuality, for example, can find their origin in this self-love. Over time, frequent encounters driven solely by selfish desires can lead to what might be called the search for the organic self.

Senseless sexual activity rejects the valuable contribution of the opposite sex: here, only a selfish form of sexuality is valued.

A married person who seeks only pleasure will, sooner or later, lose meaning in the relationship and turn to pornography or others in search of what is missing. It is a very unpleasant path, one I would not wish on anyone: the outcome, simply put, is sadness.

Complementarity

We have already seen that stimuli and desire differ between men and women. At times, they may even appear opposed or incompatible—you can see the extreme of this apparent incompatibility reflected in certain strands of the feminist movement.[63]

So where do men and women meet—and find comfort—in their desire for each other? Aren't differences between the two sexes striking?

For sexuality to make sense, physical complementarity must exist. Only a man and a woman can truly complement each other—organically and emotionally—in the giving of themselves for love. And for complementarity to bear fruit, it must follow nature.

Without complementarity, sexual relationships lose their meaning. The person who indulges in disorderly sexual activity eventually loses sight of the real perspective of who he or she is: their identity.

Fig. 34. "Tenderness is only found in the affectionate embrace of the one I love."

Our discussion now reaches a kind of climax: we all carry within us a principle of selfishness. Some are unaware of it; most recognize it. Aren't we often selfish in our attitudes and thoughts?

Don't we sometimes lack generosity, commitment, eagerness, or dedication? We procrastinate, give up easily, grow lazy, and seek comfort instead of challenge. We put ourselves first, while criticizing others as better looking, more intelligent, more capable, or more lovable. We hide our misery and justify our wrongdoings. How can a relationship thrive in such a stormy environment?

Out of fear, many turn to live-in situations. Yet these experiments fall short for several reasons:

1. The partner is used, not loved—treated more like an appliance than a person.

2. There is no proof of love—no commitment, no rights, no duties.

3. There is no fruit of love—a lack of maturity and no openness to life.

Our condition—our sexuality—is key. Perhaps it is the most vulnerable part of our nature. Sexuality is as beautiful as a piece of exquisite Chinese porcelain, and just as fragile.

Chapter Five: The Broken Jar

Pottery has come a long way before us. Even today, automation cannot match the skill of the artist—unique in communicating beauty and imparting that delicate touch to every piece that leaves the workshop.

Fig. 35. To be this beautiful is to be vulnerable.

Each work of art adds a kind of spiritual glow to the beholder. We want to possess it for what it inspires in us.

We treat every piece of art with care and respect. For centuries, wedding gifts have favored Chinese porcelain, which has remained with couples in the best and most prominent place in the home for a lifetime.

Soccer was king in our house. My father used to watch—and support with his presence—every match played by the Valencia soccer team; I often joined him in the bleachers.

We, brothers and sisters, had discovered that the ten-meter corridor at the entrance of the house was perfect for short ball practice whenever our parents were not around.

Fig. 36. We all watched the ball sail through the air in slow motion toward the precious jar.

Unfortunately, the corridor displayed a beautiful piece of Chinese porcelain on top of a side table—a monument to our parents' commitment, which had carried the six of us forward in their love for each other.

Passing the ball from one end of the corridor to the other was not difficult—it wasn't our first time, and we relied heavily on our skills as players. I think I was the one who accidentally kicked the ball "south," below the midline, and the game stopped: we all watched the ball sail through the air in slow motion toward the precious jar, tracing a perfect parabola, as if intentional—which, of course, it wasn't.

I still remember the sound the jar made as it crashed onto the floor of the corridor: the famous art piece, the symbol of my parents' commitment to each other, disintegrating into dust. Years later I learned that the most valuable porcelain pieces shatter irreparably when struck hard.

Aren't we—each one of us, no matter what race we belong to, what continent has held us, or what fortunate or unfortunate condition we find ourselves in—a precious piece of porcelain?

We can also break down, at times irreparably when circumstances lead us, voluntarily or involuntarily, to a critical point.

Repairs

Human nature—not animal nature—finds meaning in a sexual relationship only under very particular conditions. When men and women meet those conditions, they complement each other and discover a deeper purpose in their relationship. This situation, which may seem to make us fragile, is in fact our safety net.

That safety net is the commitment to a lifelong marriage. This total self-giving can transform the relationship into an overwhelming and joyful experience, drawing the couple into a unique world of love, happiness, tenderness, and contentment that cannot be found elsewhere. Only within the respect, secrecy, and privacy of marriage does the couple's empowerment truly bloom.

Fig. 37. In the circus of life, wisdom is the net we weave before the first step onto the wire.

A happy marriage is built on true love—a selfless love that desires, first, the good of the other person. The test of love is found in cherishing the fruits of that union. "Are you referring to children?" What else? Pets? A booming business? It may sound surprising to some, but yes, we are talking about children.

Much can be said about the relationship and the conditions that lead to a happy marriage—though that is not the purpose of these pages. Still, I invite you to deepen your understanding by reading *Should I Marry? The Complete Guide to Discernment*, also part of *The Big-Question Series*.

But what else can we say about safety nets?

Since English is not my native language—Spanish is—I initially thought of this "safety net" as "safe sex," which, feeling uncomfortable, I quickly set aside. Still, I turned to my favorite online thesaurus to explore the idea further. (By the way, I would like to acknowledge that *Word Hippo* has enlightened my writing innumerable times.)

I found that the closest synonyms expanding the meaning of "safety net" are *protection, assurance, deterrent, defense,* and *armor*—quite different from the net used by aerialists in a circus.

To *protect* ourselves from today's sexually aggressive environment and to *strengthen* marriage even more, we need the *armor* of *control*.

Control is necessary if we want to keep ourselves from distorting our sexuality. And control is exercised through the senses.

No advice is stronger, more direct, or more compelling—perhaps even shocking—than the words of Jesus Christ in the Bible: "You have heard that it was said, 'You shall not commit adultery.' But I say to you that everyone who looks at a woman with lust has already committed adultery with her in his heart."[64]

Uncontrolled sexual desires are stirred in the heart and enter through the senses. Adulterous desires are born this way. Adultery is considered immoral in every religion and culture, under any philosophical or fashionable ideology. We will not explore the reasons behind this here—perhaps in another publication—but the man or woman who commits adultery is universally accountable for their actions and subject to judgment. Why, then, should we not keep our desires under control?

Stoic philosophy, which emphasizes rationality, self-control, and virtue, consistently advocates moderating all impulses, including sexual ones. Epictetus' *Discourses and Enchiridion* advise us to manage our desires. Seneca's letters and essays encourage moderation, and Marcus Aurelius' *Meditations* remind us to guide our impulses and preserve inner virtue.[65]

Men from other religions—Buddhists, Muslims—have long recognized the need to govern their instincts. Christians add another dimension to this human and practical approach: the belief that God's strength to master one's passions is a gift, a grace, freely given to those who ask. "The moral law is God's fatherly instruction, guiding humanity toward happiness and away from evil."[66]

Ultimately, sexuality intertwines with intimacy to shape our identity. "In a certain sense, sex is the secret of the individual. Every disclosure of sex is the revelation of something intimate and personal"[67] Sexuality is the power within us.

The Magic in Me

In the final scenes of the musical comedy *Pitch Perfect* (2012), the climax revolves around the national 'A Capella' competition in which the Barden Bellas struggled with the Barden Trebles to deliver the most powerful and emotionally charged performance to win. The film follows Beca (Anna Kendrick), a freshman who joins the group and helps them find their unique sound while navigating college life and relationships.

In terms of sales, *Pitch Perfect* was a commercial success. It grossed over $115 million worldwide against a production budget of around $17 million. Its success led to two sequels, further cementing its popularity.

The Trebles sing...

I've got the magic in me (I've got the magic, baby)

Every time I touch that track it turns it into gold (Oh yes, it turns to gold)

Everybody knows I've got the magic, magic, magic

Magic, magic, magic, Magic, magic, magic

I've got the magic in me!

The magic within each of us is what defines who we are: it is this magic that turns everything into gold. Our inner magic is born from the essence of our sexuality.

When we talk about sexuality, we often reduce it to pleasure, but its role in our lives goes much deeper. A man isn't defined only by desire; he grows into many roles—father, partner, colleague, brother. People look to him for steadiness, for a kind of authority that comes from love rather than force. He's expected to be strong yet gentle, reliable yet courageous, someone who can guide without dominating.

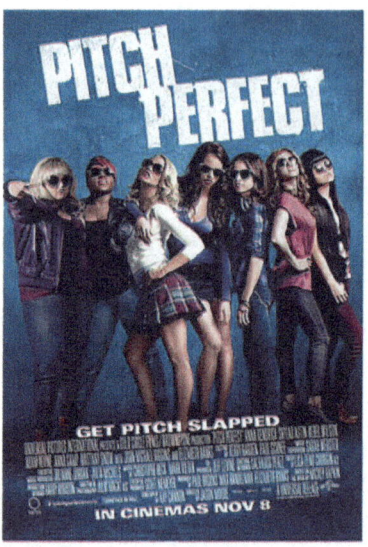

Fig. 38. *I've got the magic in me!*

A woman, in her own way, brings a warmth and tenderness that society desperately needs. Whether she appears as a mother, a partner, a sister, a friend, or a coworker, her presence often carries empathy, emotional support, and care. These qualities aren't small things; they're the glue that holds communities together.

Both men and women face the challenge of becoming who they're meant to be, and much of that growth comes from the quiet magic we carry inside us—the energy, creativity, and vitality that sexuality awakens. As this inner force shapes individuals, it also builds our world, for society itself is formed from the contributions of both sexes, each offering something the other cannot replace. Together, their influence touches every aspect of life, making it magical.

Magical

Recent research published in *NeuroImage* used dual electroencephalography (EEG) to observe the brain activity of mothers and their babies as they interacted.

What the scientists found is astonishing: the rhythms of their brains tend to synchronize, forming what some researchers describe as a kind of shared "mega-network." [68]

This interpersonal neural connectivity becomes even stronger when mothers express warmth, joy, and positive emotion. In those moments, communication flows more easily, and the child's developing brain absorbs the world with remarkable efficiency.

To contemplate this is to feel that sexuality is not merely a biological function but a gift—an opening into something far more intricate than we can fully grasp.

The complexity of gestation exceeds our understanding; it feels less like an accident of nature and more like a profound design woven into the fabric of life.

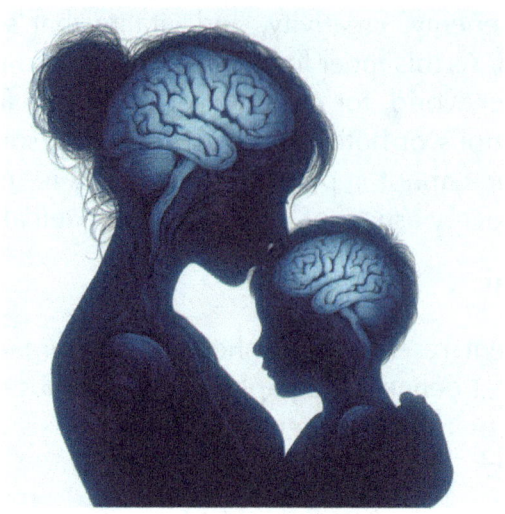

Fig. 39. The magical expression of human love.

It is difficult to describe the feeling that such an image evokes. There is something almost magical in the idea that two brains—one new to the world, one welcoming it—can fall into rhythm with each other.

The intimacy of this connection begins long before birth, and in many ways it never fully disappears. It shapes the quiet intuitions mothers often have: the sense of what their child is feeling, the subtle recognition of their joys and fears, the glimpse of who they may one day become.

And when we pause to consider it all—the warmth of a mother's intuition, the steady presence of a father's care, the mysterious rhythm that binds parent and child—we glimpse the miracle at the heart of life. Life itself is not only sustained but celebrated in these bonds, reminding us that motherhood and fatherhood are among the most beautiful expressions of what it means to be human.

Chapter Six: We Need Answers

The following sections are thematically separated to attempt further understanding and summarize the content of your readings. You will find questions here related to our conversation to help guide your reflection.

Margaret Sanger and the Sexual Liberation of Women

What can you say about Margaret Sanger?

The life of Margaret talks about a type of personality that shows in her resolution and dedication a determination in many ways commendable. It is unfortunately what she lacked was a better understanding of her concerns and the necessary anthropological background to self-criticize her methods.

Margaret Sanger's story begins with a woman who died because of self-induced abortion. Isn't it that we are talking about the safety of women?

Women are not safer through the contraceptive alternative: they are safer through healthcare services and education—this is what Margaret would have needed most. Contraceptives bring injustice to the poor as well as to the women who, without alternatives and reasons, are encouraged to use them.

How about life? How about abortion?

Don't we all need to defend life? The woman that does not respect the life-giving power within her, promotes death. The defense of life is not the focus of this book; it will be treated separately in other publications.

In the opinion of most supporters of Margaret Sanger's campaign, there was a need for the sexual liberation of women. Wasn't it necessary?

We are talking about two different things here: sexual liberation and women's rights. Women needed to equal men in their rights to intervene in society, but this is in no context related to sexuality. And sex didn't require liberation because it had never been in prison. Sexual liberation was a fallacy that would shape a senseless sexual revolution years later. The contraceptive mentality created the link.

The Contraceptive Mentality and the Poor

We often see in developing countries levels of poverty that bring many—even religious groups—to think that contraceptives are justifiable. What can you say about it? The facts are so obvious!

Do you agree with those who say that to eradicate poverty, you must eradicate the poor? Isn't it a totalitarian solution? What rights do the poor have? Injustice is not the solution to a problem that should be the concern of every human being on this planet: the end does not justify the means. Contraceptive is an injustice to those who are not given the right to be born because they are poor.

Where is the solution then?

The solution is education—which is more expensive than contraceptives, still affordable. 'The poor' becomes the excuse for those who profit from circumstances like corruption—a widespread cancer, without implying that every country in the world is suffering from it.

In some countries, poverty is so widespread that educational or development programs become impossible to achieve. What could the alternative be?

Where have you gotten that info? The alternative to educational programs is freedom. Let everyone with a right to live find his or her way in society. Did you notice that most of the ordinary services that you enjoy come to you from the hands of people living in poor neighborhoods? I haven't seen any Marchioness serving the tables in a restaurant.

You talk about freedom but see how drug addiction, crime, prostitution, and all times of maladies grow in populated areas. Isn't this the result of an abuse of freedom?

What type of populated areas are you talking about? Can you be more specific? There are densely populated but developed societies where freedom brings about law and order.

I am talking about poor districts and squatter areas where crime controls the streets.

Abuse is at the root of these problems, but who is the abuser? It is a complex issue that should be studied by those with the authority to intervene. Demagogy is often at play to excuse services and responsibilities.

How about the overpopulation of a world that might not be enough to accommodate all of us?

No study can be completed on the incredible number of unknowns and variables that could support the fantasies promoted by lobbyists and the brainwashing of, for example, the Neo-Malthusian theories. Demagogy seems to be at play again.

This question is often brought up in discussion, isn't it that an overpopulated world is affecting the earth's cycles and the environment?

Everyone should care for the environment. However, what are the agendas of the modern prophets who tell us that the world is ending? It might happen but by the earth's regular cycles. If eons ago an asteroid crashing into the earth did not pulverize it, what would? Here we can use the well-known advice of doctors: treat the symptoms. *Work-in-progress* should be the mantra of political bodies and managers who want to solve problems, not contraceptive slogans to cut down on population.

The Sexual Revolution

If the influence of people like Alfred Kinsey and others culminated in a sexual revolution brought about by contraceptives, wasn't the liberation of sex necessary?

We talked about this earlier: sex was never in prison. What the sexual revolution brought about was sexual anarchy, not liberation. Promiscuity became the norm to excuse every sexual responsibility.

Why is sexual responsibility so important?

Responsibility is only possible in humans, not in animals. Every man or woman must account for his or her actions in society. Sexual responsibility is also a human responsibility.

What makes human sexuality different from animal sexuality?

Reason[69] makes human sexuality different from animal sexuality: human sexuality is founded on reasons for love.

But in a way, we can say that animal sexuality is founded on love too. What's the difference?

Sexual attraction in animals is often confused with love: animals follow instinct only. Humans love for a reason not just instinctively.

Any function in the body can be nullified or expanded temporarily by artificial means, like using ear plugs or pressing your nose, why not using contraceptives?

It is not how but why would you do something like that? If pleasure is the only reason that comes to your mind, what you mean and I understand is 'sex free of charge.' Don't tell me that it is love because love is unconditional.

What is the reason behind human love?

Unlike animals, who simply follow instinct without proofs, our choice to love one person above all others is factual. In the end, what stronger proof could there be than saying, "Out of everyone, I choose you"?

What kind of proof lies in exclusivity?

For humans, the proof of true love is a commitment sealed by a contract. We may say "I love you," but we prove it only when we're willing to complicate our lives for that love.

So, if the reason behind human sexuality is the sake of the person we love, what is left of the sexual life in humans?

Human sexuality implies sexual unity which comes naturally as a manifestation of love: the gift of each other follows nature and is creative, not fruitless. Contraceptives get in the way and change the values of the sexual act.

Do you mean that the use of contraceptives to avoid pregnancies in the woman is detrimental to human love?

Artificial contraceptives show violence and violate love. Every organ fulfills its purpose in a specific functional way. When used differently, we only harvest frustration. Many examples can be given to illustrate that. For example, feeding a person with a tube through the nose or releasing body fluids through catheters is just frustrating and annoying. Through contraceptives, human love is misused and frustrated.

But a couple could decide to postpone their children for important reasons, doesn't it justify the use of contraceptives?

The human condition has a natural contraceptive: the woman's periodic cycles. Periodic cycles are part of human nature and make the sexual act responsible—following nature, not betraying it.

☐☐☐☐☐☐☐☐☐☐☐☐☐☐☐☐☐

Homosexuality

I am not a homosexual, but I have some friends who are, and I would like to speak for them. What should the right attitude of anyone towards homosexuality be?

No one claiming understanding of sexuality in general can have anything against anyone. It is a complicated issue that demands a deeper understanding of human nature and the environment. Despite its challenges, it should be approached with respect.

What is this 'understanding of human nature' that we are missing?

If you go over the physical, psychological, and environmental facts given in Chapter Three you can fit homosexuality in every human historical period. However, homosexuality gained more public attention in historical eras that witnessed a rise in sexual promiscuity and abuse—as documented in the last centuries of the Roman Empire. For example, Julius Caesar and Alexander the Great had intercourse with men as well as with women. They belong to a historical period that fostered indiscriminate sexual relationships. We could go on and on talking about other countries where sexual overdrive brought confusion and encouraged promiscuity. The same is happening today.

If so, is homosexuality a byproduct of circumstances?

Yes, it is. Any scientist looking into the genetic or hormonal side of it would agree. But most scientists, psychologists, and psychiatrists won't tell you that these tendencies can often change. Doctors and researchers have the tools to help with that, but they rarely volunteer the information.

Why not?

The scientific world is afraid of lobbying homosexual groups due to the widespread campaigns to push for legal recognition. Conversely, homosexuals are comfortable with their status and don't want to change. Some people would have wanted to change their situation if they knew it was possible; that's where unfairness lies. Everyone deserves the chance to fully understand their options so they can make the best decision for their own lives.

Magic

Lastly, how do we rediscover the magic within us?

The magic within us is, in essence, our sexuality. As men and women, we enrich the lives of those around us simply by being who we are—for we are made for love. We need to reflect on our contribution and how to fulfill it, for our sexuality has the power to turn everything into gold.

Conclusion

Creeping plants and climbers can be categorized by the type of damage they cause to buildings, structures, and surrounding landscaping. The most destructive species often combine rapid growth with aggressive attachment methods, such as aerial roots, suckers, or twining stems that wedge into existing cracks.

Fig. 40. Like a garden left untended, unchecked impulses can overgrow and conceal the harmony we are meant to cultivate.

Their destructive mechanisms distinguish three groups: self-climbers (which damage paint or mortar), light-fleeing species (negatively phototropic, with shoots that move into cracks and crevices), and twiners (which can strangle or pull down structures).

Every chapter in this book describes a particular situation, outlining a destructive, exaggerated drive carried out in a manner analogous to the damaging effect of a creeping plant.

We have spoken about the fast-growing pornography that spreads through the crevices of the Internet; about the structural damage caused by certain ideologies and by the careless use of contraceptives; and about the culture and customs that slowly modify our behavior, strangling our identity and turning us into something unrecognizable.

I want to emphasize that we must fight back. We should imitate the gardener who cares for every plant in the garden, trims and beautifies what he has planted, and uproots without mercy any creeping plant along with the weeds he recognizes as harmful.

Recognition is the key. Perhaps one reading of this book will not be enough. We may need to return to it several times to acknowledge our errors and to understand the risks.

A final review can help us attend to the details and strengthen our resolve to fight back.

Tex

About the Author

The author–by the nickname of Tex, obtained a Licentiate in Biology with a specialization in Zoology from the State University of Valencia, Spain. He also completed a Certificate in Education at the University of Alicante, which qualified him for teaching positions. Additionally, he holds a Diploma in Affectivity and Sexuality from the University of Navarre in Spain.

In the Philippines he ventured into other fields to add to his humanistic and technical formation finishing a master's in library and information sciences by the University of the Philippines in Diliman, that he completed with a sub specialty in library software and history and the publication of articles in specialized journals together with the printing of the book *History of Books and Libraries in the Philippines, 1521-1900*. He has also published software for library management.

He has occupied management positions in cultural centers, lectured extensively about value education, engaged in school consultancies, mentoring, and counseling. He is an avid cyclist and motorist and has been everywhere North to South in the Philippines.

Other Works by the Author

Tex Hernandez is the author of several thought-provoking books that explore some of life's biggest questions—touching on values like personal growth, relationships, identity, and decision-making. His works are brought together under the engaging umbrella of *The Big-Question Series*, with each title offering a fresh take on challenges we all face.

Am I an Atheist? Science, Atheism, and the Way of Friendship – A thoughtful look at the relationship between science and belief, and how both shape the way we connect with others.

Should I Marry? The Essential Guide to Discernment – A guide to understanding what makes commitment meaningful and how it relates to happiness and lasting success.

Shall I Dress It? Sexuality in Overdrive – An eye-opening examination of the powerful pull of sexuality, including perspectives on addiction and identity.

What Are My Chances? Life Management Explained – A practical and inspiring guide to navigating life's choices and finding a sense of purpose through planning.

Why Character? The Quest That Matters – The newest addition, offering fresh insights into character development through five essential pillars.

All titles in *The Big-Question Series* are available online via Google Play Books and Amazon Kindle.

Notes

[1] Taylor Ardrey, 'A top Spanish court ruled that a man has the right to walk around naked,' *Insider (Yahoo!News)*, February 5, 2023 (https://uk.news.yahoo.com/top-spanish-court-ruled-man-210251060.html).

[2] ChatGPT, responses to 'Nudists beach resorts in Europe,' August 2024.

[3] Taylor Ardrey, 'A top-Spanish court'.

[4] Malcom Reed, 'The Origins and Evolution of Fashion: A Cultural History,' *Edvigo*, 2024 (https://edvigo.com/humanities/).

[5] Various articles, 'Exploring Medieval Fashion Trends,' July 2024 (www.medievalists.net).

[6] Genesis 3:11

[7] James P. Bernard, 'A Brief History of Synthetic Dyes,' *First Source Worldwide, LLC (FSW)*, July 16, 2018 (https://fsw.cc/synthetic-dyes-history/).

[8] Wikipedia, 'The Sewing Machine,' September 19, 2024 (wikipedia.org).

[9] The Click Americana Team, 'Fashion history timeline,' *Click Americana*, May 2, 2024 (ttps://clickamericana.com/topics/beauty-fashion/ vintage-clothing/dress-styles-fashion-history-timeline).

[10] *Ibid.*

[11] Wikipedia, 'Margaret Sanger,' July 2024 (wikipedia.org).

[12] *Ibid.*

[13] It was after the trip of Freud and Carl Jung to the USA in 1909, when Freud's name started sounding among men of the

medical profession. However, his research only became widely known after the publication of *Introductory Lectures on Psychoanalysis* at the University of Vienna in 1919 (Eleanor Sawbridge Burton, 'Sigmund Freud,' *Institute of Psychoanalysis*, 2015, https://psychoanalysis.org.uk/).

[14] Theodore M. Brown and Elizabeth Fee, 'Alfred C. Kinsey: A Pioneer Of Sex Research,' *The National Library of Medicine*, June 2003 (https://www.ncbi.nlm.nih.gov/pmc/articles/).

[15] *Ibid.*

[16] *Ibid.* Theodore M. Brown and another publication, Teresa R. Wagne, 'Alfred Kinsey's Research Has Undermined Sexual Morality,' in Mary E. Willians, 'Sex Opposing Viewpoints' (San Diego, California: Greenhaven Press, 2000).

[17] Wikipedia, 'Alfred Kinsey,' July 2024 (wikipedia.org).

[18] William F. Jasper, 'Normalizing Child Rape: The Decades-long Kinsey-Rockefeller-Playboy Push That Produced Our Current Pedophile Crisis,' *The New American*, July 20, 2023 (https://thenewamerican.com/us/culture/normalizing-child-rape-the-decades-long-kinsey-rockefeller-playboy-push-that-produced-our-current-pedophile-crisis/).

[19] Jonathon Van Maren, 'The Forgotten and Misunderstood History of the Sexual Revolution,' October 6, 2020 (thebridgehead.ca/2020/10/06/the-forgotten-and-misunderstood-history-of-the-sexual-revolution/) and John Whitehead, 'Kinsey and the Sexual Revolution: Fifty-Five Years Later,' *The Rutherford Institute*, September 22, 2003 (www.rutherford.org).

[20] Mark Powell, 'Kinsey and Hef," *The Spectator;* cartoonist, Ben R. Daws (https://www.spectator.com.au/2017/10/kinsey-and-hef/).

[21] Gary Wilson, *Your Brain on Porn: Internet Pornography and the Emerging Science of Addiction* (North Charleston, South Carolina: Commonwealth Publishing, 2014).

[22] WifiTalents Reports, 'Sex Industry Statistics,' June 2, 2025 (https://wifitalents.com/sex-industry-statistics/).

²³ *Ibid.*

²⁴ ChatGPT, responses to 'The Matrix,' September 5, 2024.

²⁵ *Ibid.*, Introduction.

²⁶ Victoria L. Dunckley, 'Gray Matters: Too Much Screen Time Damages the Brain,' Psychology Today, February 27, 2014 (psychologytoday.com).

²⁷ Kristen A. Jenson, 'Can Using Porn Physically Change the Brain? Neurosurgeon Breaks It Down,' *Defend Young Minds*, July 11, 2022 (defendyoungminds.com).

²⁸ Gary Wilson, *Your Brain on Porn*, Foreword.

²⁹ *Ibid.*, p. 67.

³⁰ Tara Berman, MD, 'Sexual Addiction May Be Real After All,' ABC News, July 11, 2014 (abcnews.go.com) in Gary Wilson, *Your Brain on Porn*, Footnote(95).

³¹ Lauren Brande, 'Women with Porn Addictions,' *American Addiction Center*, October 26, 2023 (ProjectKnow.com).

³² Gary Wilson, Your Brain on Porn, pp. 35, 65, and 75.

³³ *Ibid.*, p. 81

³⁴ Wikipedia, 'Homosexuality,' September 16, 2024 (en.wikipedia.org).

³⁵ Critical Theory (by the Frankfurt School, institutionalized by Max Horkheimer and Theodor Adorno) stems from neo-Marxist efforts to critique capitalism, instrumental reason, and power structures, with an explicitly emancipatory and political goal. Both, constructivism and postmodernism are linked to the Critical theory by their critical stand on modern, standard society with its logical and radical conclusions.

³⁶ This contrasts with positivist or realist approaches, which assume knowledge can be objectively discovered. Constructivist ethics suggests that moral truths are not discovered but constructed through rational deliberation or social processes.

37 Neel Burton, 'When Homosexuality Stopped Being a Mental Disorder,' *Psychology Today,* June 2024 (psychologytoday.com).

38 "Bieber went on to work at Yale Medical College, New York University, and starting in 1953 at the New York Medical College, where he taught a course in psychoanalysis.[1] Bieber was, along with Lionel Ovesey and Charles Socarides, one of the most influential American psychoanalysts who postulated that gay men can be treated successfully.[3] Bieber's 1962 book Homosexuality: A Psychoanalytic Study of Male Homosexuals was a counter reaction to the 1948 Kinsey Report on male sexual behavior. It remained the leading study on homosexuality until homosexuality was removed from DSM-III in 1973" ('Irving Bieber,' Wikipedia.com).

39 "Charles William Socarides (January 24, 1922 – December 25, 2005) was an American psychiatrist, psychoanalyst, physician, educator, and author. He focused much of his career on homosexuality, which he believed could be altered. He helped found the National Association for Research & Therapy of Homosexuality (NARTH) in 1992 and worked extensively with the organization until his death" ('Charles William Socarides,' Wikipedia.com).

40 Charles Socarides, *Homosexuality: A Freedom Too Far,* January 1, 1995 (https://www.amazon.com/Homosexuality-Freedom-Charles-W-Socarides/dp/0964664259).

41 Nature, NEWS, "No 'gay gene': Massive study homes in on genetic basis of human sexuality," 29 August 2019 (https://www.nature.com/articles/d41586-019-02585-6).

42 Bennett McIntosh, *Science, Harvard Magazine,* "There's (Still) No Gay Gene," August 29, 2019 (https://www.harvardmagazine.com/2019/08/there-s-still-no-gay-gene).

43 The Huberman Lab Podcast, 'Biological Influences On Sex, Sex Differences & Preferences,' Podcast #14 by Andrew Huberman, professor of Neurobiology and Ophthalmology at Stanford School of Medicine.

[44] We are perhaps ignoring the fact that the development of the brain is much more complex than the endocrine system—often dependent on it. When a critical variation leading to a malfunctioning of the brain is detected the alternative is branded a neurodegenerative disease, disorder, or syndrome, not a normal, functional, and natural condition. And so, any hereditary, congenital, or hormonal imbalance in the endocrine system should be similarly categorized. The processes involved in brain development are generally considered more complex than those of the endocrine system. Brain development involves intricate patterns of cellular proliferation, migration, differentiation, and synaptogenesis, as well as the establishment of neural circuits and connections. This complexity is influenced by genetic, environmental, and experiential factors. In contrast, while the development of the endocrine system is also intricate—requiring the formation of glands and the regulation of hormone production—its processes are often more straightforward in comparison. The endocrine system primarily involves the differentiation of specific cell types and the production of hormones that regulate various bodily functions (ChatGPT, responses to 'Complexity in brain development compared to the development of the endocrine system,' October 5, 2024).

[45] A synthesis of the complex research summarized by Copilot indicates that Swift-Gallant et al., in one of the most comprehensive peer-reviewed articles to date, conclude that sexual orientation is organized during prenatal development rather than altered by later-life hormonal fluctuations. In their review, postnatal hormonal imbalance — even when caused by external agents — is not shown to 'change' an individual's sexual orientation (Ashlyn Swift-Gallant et al., *Springer Nature*, "Organizational Effects of Gonadal Hormones on Human Sexual Orientation," 20 September 2023; https://link.springer.com/article/10.1007/s40750-023-00226-x).

[16] Guevedoces in the town of Las Salinas have an occurrence ratio of 1 of every 90 unaffected males. It is high but limited to a specific geographical area. AIS is an uncommon and rare

genetic condition. The CAIS variation is present in 1 among 20,000 to 50,000 people who are genetically male. Guevedoces, as a rare condition, may appear more frequently in isolated populations where consanguineous (within-family) marriages are more common (*Wikipedia*, 'Androgen Insensitivity Syndrome,' September 6, 2024).

[47] The lobbying of groups like the Human Rights Campaign (HRC) in the United States, Stonewall in the UK, the International Lesbian, Gay, Bisexual, Trans and Intersex Association (ILGA), the Lambda Legal, the OutRight Action International, and the Global Action for Trans Equality (GATE) are pushing agendas to justify their existence and pressure changes in legislation.

[48] Gary Wilson, *Your Brain on Porn*, p. 48.

[49] *Ibid.*

[50] *Ibid.*, p. 90.

[51] Julian D. Ford, 'A Developmental Trauma Perspective on Childhood Sexual Abuse,' September 22, 2020 (jamanetwork.com).

[52] In my conversation with people of all ages over the years, the homosexual issues brought about as problems have often originated from traumatic child abuse experiences.

[53] Sana Ali, Saadia Anwar Pasha, Ann Cox & Enaam Youssef, 'Examining the short and long-term impacts of child sexual abuse: a review study,' February 15, 2024 (link.springer.com).

[54] Helen Vlasova, 'The State of Sex Education (Statistics & Facts – 2024),' January 29, 2023 (admissionsly.com/sex-education-statistics).

[55] Open Secrets, 'Industry Profile: Gay & lesbian rights & issues' (opensecrets.org/federal-lobbying); and Jo Yurkaba, 'Over 30 new LGBTQ education laws are in effect as students go back to school,' August 31, 2023 (nbcnews.com/nbc-out/out-politics-and-policy/30-new-lgbtq-education-laws-are-effect-students-go-back-school-rcna101897).

[56] DSWD, 'DSWD leads signing of IRR of Parent Effectiveness Service Program Act,' June 15 and July 28, 2022 (fo3.dswd.gov.ph/2023/06/).

[57] Cormac Burke, *Covenanted Happiness*, Third Edition (The United Kingdom: The Dunstan Trust, 2019), 'Sexuality and Sexual Identity,' p. 18.

[58] Conversation with Copilot prompted by the author's inquiry describing Bernini's Apollo and Daphne sculptures.

[59] Various Authors, "A study of sexual assault: Based on data from Boramae One-stop Service Center," January 2010 (https://www.researchgate.net/publication/267566953_A_study_of_sexual_assault_Based_on_data_from_Boramae_One-stop_Service_Center).

[60] Hertenstein, M. J., Holmes, R., McCullough, M., & Keltner, D. (2009). "The communication of emotion via touch." *Emotion*, 9(4), 566-573 (https://psycnet.apa.org/doiLanding?doi=10.1037%2Fa0016107).

[61] Located in a cave site in Morocco, these fossils were first discovered in the 1960s. Initially thought to be around 40,000 years old, 2017 research utilized thermoluminescence dating to reveal they are approximately 315,000 years old (See Wikipedia, 'Jebel Irhoud').

[62] Gemini, responses to 'The reality show Naked and Afraid,' September 24, 2024.

[63] Feminism as a radical movement is traced to Marxist ideology and the Critical Theory. The radical opposition and rejection of the male contribution to the female is seen as a form of struggle from which, according to Marxist theories, something better will emerge.

[64] Gospel of Saint Mathew, Chapter 5, verses 27-28.

[65] Copilot, responses to 'Stoic philosophers on sexual moderation,' October 8, 2024.

[66] Catechism of the Catholic Church, 'The Moral Law' (https://www.vatican.va/content/catechism/en/part_three/section_one/chapter_three/article_1.html).

[67] Dietrich von Hildebrand, *Man and Woman* (Manchester, New Hampshire: Sophia Institute Press, 1992), 'Men and women differ essentially,' p. 29.

[68] *University of Cambridge*, "Mothers' and babies' brains 'more in tune' when mother is happy," 2019 (https://www.cam.ac.uk/research/news/mothers-and-babies-brains-more-in-tune-when-mother-is-happy).

[69] Reason is different from intelligence; intelligence is a capacity, reason is self-awareness.

Made in the USA
Coppell, TX
28 February 2026

72589646R00075